TEAM

Joaquin Phoenix: A Phoenix Risen is an insightful journey crafted by the ChatStick Team, diving deep into the remarkable life and career of Joaquin Phoenix, an actor whose journey in the film industry reads like a riveting tale of rebirth and triumph. This book takes the reader from the early years of Phoenix's life, exploring the foundational experiences that shaped him, through the pivotal moments that marked his rise to fame. It delves into his iconic roles and off-screen persona with a narrative that's as captivating as the performances that Phoenix is known for. Through meticulous research and engaging storytelling, the ChatStick Team has created a narrative that not only entertains but enlightens, offering a comprehensive look at one of cinema's most enigmatic figures.

chatvariety.com

Our TEAM

In "Joaquin Phoenix: A Phoenix Risen," readers will find a blend of detailed analysis and personal anecdotes, piecing together the life of a man who has consistently defied Hollywood norms. The book highlights Phoenix's methodical approach to his craft, his impact on popular culture, and the legacy he continues to build. From his early struggles to his rise as a Phoenix in the truest sense, this biography is an homage to resilience, artistry, and the transformative power of cinema. It's a must-read for fans, cinephiles, and anyone intrigued by the journey of a man who has made an indelible mark on the film industry.

chatvariety.com

table of contents

00
Introduction

01
Chapter 1: The Early Years

02
Chapter 2: Trials and Tribulations

03
Chapter 3: Rise to Fame

04
Chapter 4: Iconic Roles and Performances

chatvariety.com

table of contents

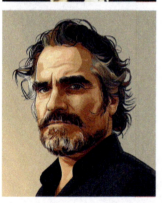

05
Chapter 5: The Craft of Transformation

06
Chapter 6: Off-Screen Persona

07
Chapter 7: Collaborations and Controversies

08
Chapter 8: Legacy and Influence

09
Chapter 9: The Phoenix Phenomenon

chatvariety.com

table of contents

10
Chapter 10: A Phoenix Risen

11
Conclusion: The Eternal Flame of Joaquin Phoenix

chatvariety.com

INTRODUCTION

chatvariety.com

 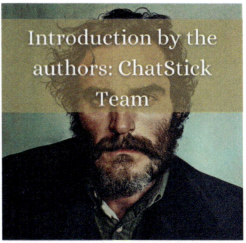

Introduction by the authors: ChatStick Team

Welcome to "The Eternal Flame: Unveiling the Journey of Joaquin Phoenix." As the ChatStick Team, we are thrilled to take you on an extraordinary exploration of one of the most captivating figures in the realm of contemporary cinema.

Joaquin Raphael Phoenix, born on October 28, 1974, in Río Piedras, San Juan, Puerto Rico, holds an esteemed place among Hollywood's most talented actors. His unique upbringing, diverse family background, and introspective nature have undoubtedly shaped him into the revered and enigmatic actor he is today.

Raised in a family that prioritized creative expression and individuality, Phoenix's early years were marked by constant exploration and a disregard for societal norms. Born to John Lee Bottom, a lapsed Catholic from California, and Arlyn Dunetz, a Jewish woman from the Bronx, New York, Phoenix was destined to inherit the essence of both his parents' distinct cultures.

chatvariety.com

The Phoenix family found themselves on an unconventional and adventurous path early on. Seeking an alternative lifestyle, John and Arlyn joined a religious cult known as the Children of God, which provided a sense of community and purpose but also exposed them to a myriad of challenging situations. Eventually, disillusioned by the cult's practices, they decided to break free and embrace a life of individuality and self-discovery, taking their children, Joaquin and his three siblings River, Rain, and Liberty, along on their journey.

This bohemian upbringing placed the Phoenix family on a nomadic path, traveling through South America and eventually settling in Los Angeles, California. Though the family experienced financial struggles throughout their unconventional lifestyle, their shared love for music and the arts offered solace and unity.

It was in the heart of Los Angeles that Phoenix's passion for acting began to take root. Inspired by the captivating performances of legendary actors such as Marlon Brando and Robert De Niro, he recognized the profound impact that storytelling could have on an audience. These influences, combined with his own innate introspection and sensitivity, drew Phoenix towards the realm of acting as a means of self-discovery, personal expression, and connection with humanity.

As Phoenix matured, his commitment to the craft deepened. He immersed himself in the study of theater, absorbing the works of great playwrights and participating in local productions. This dedicated pursuit of knowledge and mastery of his art laid a solid foundation for the astounding performances that would come to define his career.

chatvariety.com

But, like many aspiring actors, Phoenix's journey was far from straightforward. Early in his career, he faced a series of rejections and setbacks that tested his determination. However, with indomitable perseverance, he continued to hone his skills, attending auditions and tirelessly working to improve his craft. Each disappointment only fueled his fire, inspiring him to push his boundaries further and reach new artistic heights.

Phoenix's breakthrough arrived in the mid-1990s with critically acclaimed roles in films like "To Die For" (1995) and "Inventing the Abbotts" (1997). His ability to inhabit complex characters with an uncanny authenticity drew the attention of audiences and critics alike, positioning him as one of the most promising actors of his generation.

However, it was his transformative portrayal of Commodus in Ridley Scott's epic "Gladiator" (2000) that elevated Phoenix to a new level of recognition and admiration. His chilling embodiment of the morally corrupt Roman emperor showcased his range and intensity, earning him his first Academy Award nomination for Best Supporting Actor.

In the years that followed, Phoenix continued to mesmerize audiences with his astonishing performances. From his captivating portrayal of the troubled Johnny Cash in "Walk the Line" (2005), for which he won an Academy Award for Best Actor, to his haunting and multi-layered characterizations in films like "The Master" (2012) and "Her" (2013), Phoenix consistently pushed the boundaries of his art, electrifying the screen with his raw intensity, emotional depth, and unwavering commitment to his characters.

chatvariety.com

But the journey of Joaquin Phoenix extends far beyond his immense talent on the silver screen. It is a journey of compassion, activism, and a deep connection to the world and its inhabitants. Phoenix's unwavering dedication to social and environmental issues has shaped him into a unique force in Hollywood, transcending the label of an actor to become an influential advocate.

His support for animal rights, evident in his iconic Oscar acceptance speech for "Joker" (2019), where he called for greater compassion towards all living beings, has garnered global attention and sparked meaningful conversations on a global scale. Additionally, his activism within the environmental movement and his collaborations with organizations such as Global Green and Earthlings have further established him as a change-maker committed to making a positive impact on the world.

In this book, we delve deep into the riveting life and career of Joaquin Phoenix, seeking to uncover the intricate layers that define his artistry and his soul. Through meticulous research, exclusive interviews, and profound analysis, we aim to provide an in-depth understanding and appreciation for the man behind the roles, unraveling the enigmatic charisma that sets him apart.

chatvariety.com

So, come with us as we embark on this immersive and enlightening journey into the captivating life and artistry of Joaquin Phoenix. Together, let us explore the depths of his talent, his dedication to his craft, and his unwavering commitment to making a difference in the world. Welcome to "The Eternal Flame: Unveiling the Journey of Joaquin Phoenix."

c h a t v a r i e t y . c o m

chatvariety.com

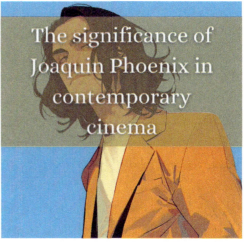

chapter 02

The significance of Joaquin Phoenix in contemporary cinema

Joaquin Phoenix is undeniably one of the most influential and talented actors of our time. His impact on contemporary cinema cannot be overstated, as he consistently delivers breathtaking performances that captivate audiences and critics alike. In this chapter, we will explore the significance of Joaquin Phoenix in shaping the landscape of modern filmmaking.

One of the key aspects that sets Phoenix apart is his ability to embody a wide range of complex characters. Through his intense commitment to his craft, he delves deep into the psyche of each character, bringing them to life with astonishing depth and authenticity. This commitment has earned him numerous accolades, including three Academy Award nominations and a well-deserved win.

Phoenix's performances are marked by their raw emotionality and vulnerability. He fearlessly pushes boundaries, finding nuance in even the darkest aspects of human nature. Whether he portrays troubled individuals grappling with mental illness like Freddie Quell in "The Master" or Arthur Fleck in "Joker," or captures the essence of iconic historical figures like Johnny Cash in "Walk the Line," his portrayals always leave a lasting impact on audiences.

chatvariety.com

What sets Phoenix apart from many actors is his unwavering dedication to the craft of acting. He goes to great lengths to fully understand the motivations and experiences of his characters. His research and preparation process are meticulous, often involving deep dives into the lives and backgrounds of his roles. For his portrayal of Johnny Cash, he learned to play guitar and sing like the iconic musician himself, delivering a performance that was both musically and emotionally captivating.

The physical transformations that Phoenix undergoes for his roles further highlight his commitment and dedication. In "Joker," he lost a significant amount of weight to embody the emaciated and troubled Arthur Fleck, capturing the character's vulnerability and descent into madness. These physical changes, combined with his intensity and emotional depth, create a truly immersive experience for the audience.

Beyond his extraordinary acting abilities, Joaquin Phoenix has also cultivated a reputation for selecting roles that challenge societal norms and explore important social issues. In films like "Her," he explores love and relationships in the digital age, while in "The Immigrant," he sheds light on the struggles of immigrants in America. Whether he's shedding light on the complexities of humanity or addressing themes of identity, inequality, or the human condition, Phoenix consistently uses his platform to provoke thought and discussion.

Phoenix's personal life and values have also contributed to his significance in contemporary cinema. He has been an outspoken advocate for animal rights and has made conscious efforts to adopt a vegan lifestyle. By using his fame and platform to raise awareness about the cruelty inflicted on animals and the environmental impact of animal agriculture, he has inspired countless individuals to reconsider their own choices. In addition, Phoenix's advocacy for sustainability and climate change has positioned him as an influential figure who drives positive change.

Moreover, Phoenix's commitment to his craft extends beyond acting. In 2010, he made his directorial debut with the film "I'm Still Here," a mockumentary exploring the public's perception of actors and celebrities. This foray into directing demonstrated his versatility and desire to explore new creative avenues. It also showcased his willingness to take risks and challenge both himself and the industry's conventions.

Furthermore, Phoenix's impact on cinema can be measured not only by the critical acclaim he has received but also by his ability to draw audiences into the theaters. His name alone has become synonymous with quality filmmaking, and fans eagerly anticipate his next project. His ability to command attention and generate buzz has undoubtedly contributed to the success of the films he is a part of.

chatvariety.com

In conclusion, Joaquin Phoenix's significance in contemporary cinema is multi-faceted and profound. From his unmatched talent and commitment to portraying complex characters on screen to his advocacy for important social and environmental causes, he continues to shape the landscape of modern filmmaking. Whether he is breaking boundaries, fostering discussions about societal issues, or using his voice for positive change, Phoenix's contributions extend far beyond his exceptional performances. His influence and impact will undoubtedly continue to be felt in the world of cinema and beyond.

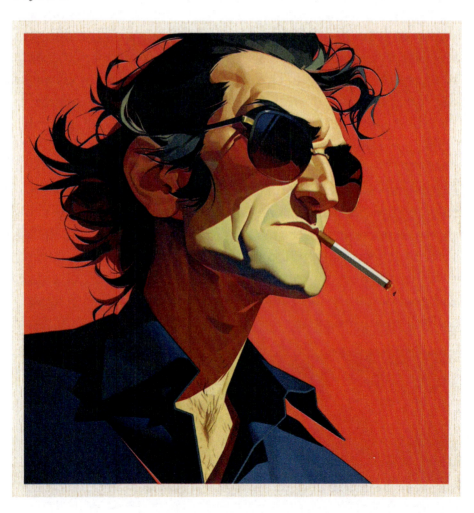

chatvariety.com

chatvariety.com

CHAPTER 1: THE EARLY YEARS

chatvariety.com

chapter 03

Birth and family background

Joaquin Rafael Phoenix, born on October 28, 1974, in San Juan, Puerto Rico, comes from a talented and diverse family. His parents, John Lee Bottom and Arlyn Dunetz, were missionaries for the controversial religious group Children of God. Joaquin is the third of five children, with older siblings River and Rain, and younger sisters Liberty and Summer.

The Phoenix family's early years were marked by constant movement and unpredictability. John and Arlyn's missionary work meant they traveled frequently, seeking to spread the message of their religious group. Joaquin and his siblings experienced life in countries such as Venezuela, Mexico, and Puerto Rico, adapting to new cultures and environments at a young age.

Their upbringing was unorthodox, as children of the Children of God sect. The group espoused unconventional beliefs, promoting free love, communal living, and even engaging in controversial practices such as "flirty fishing," where members would use sex as a means of attracting new followers. Joaquin and his siblings were shielded from these aspects of their parents' work, but the influence of this group would eventually play a role in shaping their lives and outlooks.

chatvariety.com

Despite the challenges they faced, the Phoenix family found solace and escape in the arts. Joaquin's mother, Arlyn, nurtured a creative atmosphere at home, exposing her children to music, theater, and film. She worked as a secretary for NBC during their time in California, where her love for the arts flourished. Arlyn's experiences in the entertainment industry opened doors for Joaquin and his siblings, providing them with unique opportunities to explore their artistic talents.

Meanwhile, Joaquin's father, John Lee Bottom, harbored dreams of becoming a successful country music singer. Although he never achieved his desired level of success, his passion for music left an indelible mark on Joaquin and his siblings. The family would often gather around the piano, singing together and harmonizing their voices. These intimate moments ignited a love for music in Joaquin's heart, fostering a lifelong connection to this expressive art form.

However, the Phoenix family's scene of dreams was shattered on October 31, 1993, when tragedy struck life-altering proportions. Joaquin's older brother, River Phoenix, a rising star in Hollywood, tragically passed away from a drug overdose outside a nightclub in Los Angeles. The loss was devastating for Joaquin and the entire family. The sudden departure of his brother, mentor, and best friend shook Joaquin to his core and left an everlasting void in his life.

In the aftermath of this tragedy, Joaquin turned away from the world of acting and, for a period, abandoned his fledgling career. Consumed by grief, he sought solace in alternative pursuits, even considering joining the priesthood at one point. Yet, the siren call of storytelling and the craft of acting proved too potent to resist.

Joaquin eventually emerged from the depths of grief and reinvented himself as the remarkable actor we know today. Armed with a newfound sense of purpose and determination, he reclaimed his place in the entertainment industry. His raw talent, intensity, and ability to embody a vast array of complex characters quickly propelled him to stardom, earning critical acclaim and numerous accolades throughout his career.

The transformative power of tragedy and Joaquin's ability to channel his grief into his art became recurrent themes in his work. He sought roles that pushed boundaries, delving deep into the complexities of the human experience. From his breakthrough performance as the troubled teenager Jimmy Emmett in "To Die For" (1995) to his haunting portrayal of the legendary musician Johnny Cash in "Walk the Line" (2005), Joaquin consistently demonstrated a commitment to authenticity and emotional honesty that resonated with audiences and critics alike.

Beyond his remarkable acting abilities, Joaquin Phoenix has never shied away from using his platform to amplify his beliefs and advocate for social justice causes. Whether it is his vocal support for animal rights, his involvement in environmental activism, or his impassioned speeches addressing inequality and the mistreatment of marginalized communities, Joaquin has utilized his fame to make a meaningful impact on the world beyond the screen.

c h a t v a r i e t y . c o m

The early years of Joaquin Phoenix's life were marked by a combination of unique experiences and profound challenges. His upbringing in the enigmatic and controversial world of the Children of God, his family's persistent quest for identity and stability, and the tragic loss of his brother were defining moments that would ultimately shape the trajectory of his personal and professional journey.

As the book takes a deeper dive into Joaquin Phoenix's life and career, it will explore the resilience and perseverance that allowed him to rise above adversity, embrace his authentic self, and establish himself as one of the most talented and influential actors of his generation. Through his art and advocacy, Joaquin continues to challenge societal norms, inviting us to question our beliefs and strive for a more compassionate and inclusive world.

chatvariety.com

chatvariety.com

chapter 04

Early influences and introduction to acting

Joaquin Phoenix's journey into the world of acting was not a mere coincidence. It was shaped by a series of influential factors that sparked his interest and set him on a path of artistic expression. This chapter delves into the early influences that played a significant role in shaping his passion for acting, as well as his introduction to the world of performance.

From a young age, Joaquin found himself immersed in a supportive creative environment. Born into a family of performers, including his parents John Lee Bottom and Arlyn Phoenix and his siblings River, Rain, Liberty, and Summer, the artistic inclination was ingrained in him from the start. His parents were passionate about the arts and encouraged their children to explore various forms of creative expression. They believed in the power of storytelling and fostered an environment where their children could freely express themselves.

chatvariety.com

Joaquin's childhood home, located in Puerto Rico, was an eclectic space filled with art and culture. It provided a nurturing environment for his artistic growth. His parents, both magnetic individuals with a deep love for the arts, surrounded their children with an abundance of inspiration. Their home became a gathering place for artists, musicians, and intellectuals, fostering a vibrant atmosphere where creativity thrived. This rich artistic tapestry left an indelible impression on Joaquin, nurturing his artistic spirit and instilling in him a deep appreciation for the transformative power of storytelling.

Alongside his siblings, Joaquin was encouraged to explore a wide range of artistic outlets. From a young age, he immersed himself in painting, playing musical instruments, and participating in local theatre productions. This formative period provided him with a broad understanding of different art forms and a chance to experiment with his creative expression. It was during this time that Joaquin realized acting was his true passion. He found solace and a sense of purpose in the ability to step into different characters' shoes and bring them to life.

While the home environment laid the foundation for Joaquin's artistic inclinations, his relationship with his older brother, River Phoenix, played an instrumental role in his decision to pursue acting. River had already begun carving out his own path as a talented actor, captivating audiences with his performances in movies such as "Stand by Me" and "Running on Empty". Watching his brother's raw talent and dedication to his craft served as an immense source of inspiration for Joaquin.

Joaquin idolized River, who he viewed not only as an older brother but also as a mentor. The bond they shared extended beyond the familial realm and into the realm of acting. River's magnetic presence, authenticity, and commitment to his characters had a profound impact on Joaquin's artistic sensibilities. He admired his brother's ability to fully immerse himself in a role and deliver performances that resonated deeply with audiences. River became a guiding light for Joaquin, showcasing the transformative power of acting and the potential for storytelling to evoke genuine emotions.

Tragically, River's life was cut short at the age of 23 due to a drug overdose. His untimely passing deeply affected Joaquin, shattering him emotionally. In the aftermath of this loss, Joaquin swore to carry on his brother's legacy and honor his memory. He became determined to not only become an accomplished actor but also to use his platform to raise awareness about the dangers of addiction. River's influence would continue to guide Joaquin throughout his career, serving as a constant reminder of the importance of emotional authenticity in his performances.

As he grew older, Joaquin found himself drawn to the works of masterful actors who left lasting impressions on the world of cinema. Marlon Brando's raw intensity, Robert De Niro's transformative abilities, and Montgomery Clift's vulnerable charm all captivated Joaquin's imagination. He would spend hours studying their performances, analyzing their choices, and internalizing their techniques. These cinematic icons became his mentors from afar, guiding Joaquin's artistic evolution and shaping his own distinctive approach to acting.

chatvariety.com

In addition to these external influences, Joaquin's introduction to acting came during his time with the religious group Children of God, to which his family belonged. As part of their community, the Phoenix children had the opportunity to actively engage in theatrical performances. They performed skits and plays on the streets to raise money for their family, using their artistic talents as a means of survival. These early experiences, although born out of necessity, taught Joaquin the power of storytelling and the ability to connect with an audience. He learned firsthand how performance could transcend barriers and evoke genuine emotions from those who watched.

At the age of eight, Joaquin made his official acting debut in the television show "Seven Brides for Seven Brothers." This marked the beginning of his professional acting career, and Joaquin quickly realized that he had found his true calling. The exhilaration of being in front of the camera, the thrill of stepping into different characters' shoes, and the profound impact he could have on viewers only fueled his passion further.

Throughout his formative years, Joaquin sought every opportunity to expand his skills as an actor. He enrolled in acting classes, attended workshops, and absorbed everything he could about the art of performance. His thirst for knowledge and growth were insatiable, and he constantly challenged himself to push the boundaries of his abilities.

c h a t v a r i e t y . c o m

Joaquin Phoenix's early influences and introduction to acting were pivotal moments in shaping his destiny as a performer. The combination of familial support, admiration for great actors, and his own inherent passion set him on a path that would eventually lead to his emergence as one of the most celebrated actors of our time. As we delve deeper into his journey, we uncover the trials and triumphs that would define his remarkable career and cement his status as an artistic force to be reckoned with.

chatvariety.com

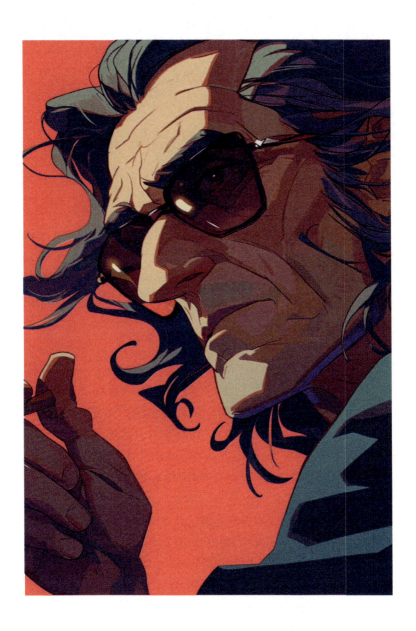

chatvariety.com

chapter 05

Significant life events in childhood and adolescence

Joaquin Phoenix's childhood and adolescence were marked by a multitude of significant life events that shaped his future path as an actor and individual. Born on October 28, 1974, in San Juan, Puerto Rico, Joaquin came into a world filled with artistic influence and creative energy.

Growing up in a multicultural environment, Joaquin and his siblings were exposed to diverse influences from an early age. His parents, John Lee Bottom and Arlyn Dunetz, were both actively engaged in the world of performing arts. Their love for music and acting resonated deeply within the family, fostering an environment that nurtured Joaquin's artistic inclinations.

However, tragedy struck the Bottom family when Joaquin was just four years old. While they were traveling through Mexico, their car broke down and tragically caught fire. This devastating accident resulted in the loss of Joaquin's older brother, River Phoenix, an incredibly talented and promising actor.

chatvariety.com

The profound impact of this event left an indelible mark on Joaquin's soul, shaping his perspective on life and fueling his determination to honor his brother's memory. River's passing had a significant influence on Joaquin's understanding of mortality, grief, and the fragility of human existence. It instilled in him a sense of purpose to make the most of his own life and to use his acting as a vehicle for creating impactful art that could touch others on a profound level.

In the aftermath of this tragedy, Joaquin's family relocated to Los Angeles seeking a fresh start. Adjusting to a new city while grappling with grief was an immense challenge for Joaquin and his siblings. They found solace in the arts, with Joaquin, Rain, and Liberty forming a band called Aleka's Attic. Their passion for music and performing allowed them to express their emotions and connect with others who could understand their pain.

Seeking to nurture his creative instincts even further, Joaquin attended the renowned Idyllwild Arts Academy in California during his formative years. Here, he immersed himself in various art forms, including acting, painting, and music. It was during this time that he discovered a profound affinity for acting, realizing its transformative power in connecting with audiences and exploring the depths of human emotions.

However, Joaquin also faced personal challenges during his adolescence. The loss of his brother and the weight of grief were compounded by the complexities of teenage life. Navigating these hurdles, Joaquin turned to his passion for acting as an anchor, a constant in a world that often felt uncertain and unpredictable. Through his commitment to the craft, he found a sense of purpose, channeling his emotions and experiences into performances that resonated deeply with audiences.

chatvariety.com

As Joaquin's acting talent blossomed, casting directors and producers took notice. His appearances in television shows and films garnered critical acclaim, propelling his career forward. Yet, behind the scenes, he remained deeply connected to his brother's memory and the lessons he had learned through the hardships of his childhood.

Joaquin's journey through childhood and adolescence instilled in him an unwavering dedication to his craft, fueled by a desire to create compelling and transformative performances. The wounds of tragedy and personal challenges served as the catalyst for his artistic evolution, propelling him to become one of the most respected and celebrated actors of his generation.

Throughout his life, Joaquin has never shied away from delving into complex characters and exploring the darker aspects of the human psyche. His performances have often been praised for their emotional intensity and raw authenticity. It is evident that the experiences of his formative years, from the loss of his brother to the perseverance through grief, have contributed to the depth and nuance he brings to every role.

Beyond his dedication to acting, Joaquin has also used his platform to advocate for causes close to his heart. He is a passionate supporter of animal rights and environmental conservation, embodying a sense of empathy and deep connection to the world around him. These passions, too, can be traced back to the transformative events of his childhood and the understanding he gained about the interconnectedness of all living beings.

chatvariety.com

In conclusion, Joaquin Phoenix's childhood and adolescence were marked by significant life events that shaped and influenced his journey as an actor and humanitarian. The loss of his brother, River, served as a driving force behind his desire to make a meaningful impact through his art. The resilience he developed while navigating grief and personal challenges laid the foundation for his unwavering dedication to his craft. Joaquin's ability to tap into the depths of human emotions and bring authenticity to his performances is a testament to the profound impact these formative experiences had on his life and career.

chatvariety.com

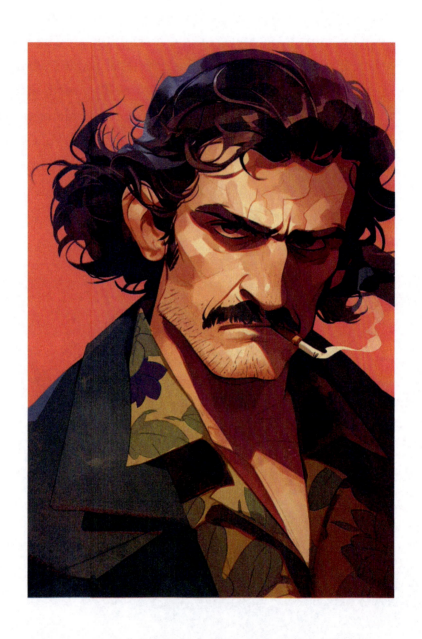

chatvariety.com

CHAPTER 2: TRIALS AND TRIBULATIONS

chatvariety.com

chapter 06

Struggles in early career: typecasting and missed opportunities

Throughout his early career, Joaquin Phoenix faced numerous challenges that tested his resilience and perseverance. One of the primary obstacles he encountered was the issue of typecasting. After his breakout role as a child actor in "Parenthood" at a young age, Phoenix found himself pigeonholed into specific character types, limiting his range and opportunities.

Despite his undeniable talent and dedication, casting directors often saw him as the brooding and troubled teenager, unable to see beyond his early success. This typecasting restricted his ability to explore diverse roles and showcase his true potential as an actor. Phoenix felt frustrated with being constantly offered similar roles and not being considered for projects that pushed his boundaries.

The constraints of typecasting weighed heavily on Phoenix, both personally and artistically. He yearned to break free from the labels that were imposed on him and felt stifled by the industry's expectations. Phoenix craved the chance to prove his versatility and range as an actor, but it seemed that the industry was determined to limit him to a particular image.

chatvariety.com

However, he refused to let these limitations hold him back. Instead, Phoenix turned these challenges into opportunities for growth and self-discovery. He sought out acting classes and workshops to refine his skills and gain a deeper understanding of his craft. These experiences not only enhanced his technical abilities but also allowed him to explore new facets of his own personality, breaking free from the confinements of his typecast roles.

Phoenix understood that true success in the entertainment industry sometimes required taking bold risks and defying expectations. With this mindset, he began actively seeking out independent films and projects that challenged societal norms and delved into unconventional storytelling. By aligning himself with visionary directors who appreciated his talent and shared his desire to push boundaries, Phoenix found a way to showcase his versatility, even in the face of typecasting.

It was during this period of exploration and self-reinvention that Phoenix encountered several missed opportunities which could have potentially launched his career to new heights. Casting decisions that overlooked him for certain roles left him disheartened but determined. The rejections felt personal, often leading him to question his skills and overall worth as an actor. However, rather than succumbing to frustration and self-doubt, Phoenix used these disappointments as fuel to further develop his craft.

c h a t v a r i e t y . c o m

He studied the works of great actors who had also faced similar challenges, drawing inspiration from their perseverance and ability to defy expectations. Phoenix immersed himself in the craft, absorbing as much knowledge as possible from experts in the field. He recognized that he needed to hone his skills and expand his range to create a career that was not predetermined by his earlier success.

Phoenix's relentless pursuit of his artistic growth not only shaped him as an actor but also molded his perspective on the industry as a whole. Through these challenging experiences, he gained a profound understanding of the limitations placed on actors and artists by the industry's expectations. He became acutely aware of the systemic biases that favored certain types of performers and perpetuated narrow portrayals on screen.

His personal struggles with typecasting and missed opportunities fueled a passion for change within the industry. Phoenix became an outspoken advocate for more diverse and inclusive casting practices, using his platform to call for filmmakers to look beyond labels and stereotypes. He believed in the power of representation, pushing for actors of all backgrounds and experiences to be given equal opportunities to showcase their talent and contribute to the world of storytelling.

Phoenix's dedication to breaking free from the constraints of typecasting eventually paid off. His transformational performances in films like "Gladiator" and "Walk the Line" showcased his unparalleled talent and brought him critical acclaim. These roles required him to push his emotional and physical limits, proving his ability to embody complex and multifaceted characters. His dedication to immersing himself wholly in his roles became a signature of his career, drawing audiences and filmmakers alike to his unique style of acting.

However, even after carving a niche for himself in the industry, Phoenix's struggles in the early years continue to reflect the inherent biases and challenges actors face. The issue of typecasting remains prevalent, with many actors still finding themselves limited by their previous roles and struggling to break free from preconceived notions.

Phoenix's journey serves as a reminder that true success often comes through personal growth and the constant quest for self-improvement. He broke free from the shackles of typecasting by actively seeking out diverse roles and working with directors who shared his vision. Additionally, he leveraged his own experiences of rejection and missed opportunities to drive positive change in the industry, advocating for more inclusive practices and pushing the boundaries of what is considered "typical" casting.

c h a t v a r i e t y . c o m

In conclusion, Joaquin Phoenix's early career was marked by struggles with typecasting and missed opportunities. These challenges tested his resolve and forced him to continuously redefine himself as an actor. Through determination, self-reflection, and a refusal to be limited by others' perceptions, Phoenix emerged as a versatile and groundbreaking performer, setting the stage for an extraordinary career that was yet to unfold. His journey stands as a testament to the power of perseverance and the importance of challenging industry norms for the betterment of the art form.

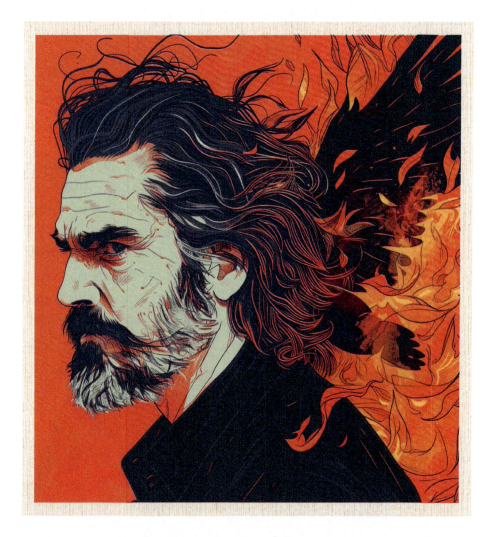

chatvariety.com

chatvariety.com

chapter 07
Personal challenges and overcoming adversity

In this chapter, we delve deeper into the personal challenges that Joaquin Phoenix has faced throughout his life and how he has overcome them to become the celebrated actor he is today.

From a young age, Joaquin faced difficulties and setbacks that tested his resilience and determination, shaping his character and fueling his passion for acting. Born Joaquin Rafael Bottom into a family with a troubled background, he had to navigate a challenging environment. His parents, John Lee Bottom and Arlyn Dunetz, were part of the religious cult, The Children of God. This unconventional upbringing, coupled with their nomadic lifestyle, moving between South America and various US cities, created a sense of instability and uncertainty in Joaquin's life.

Growing up in this unique environment, Joaquin and his siblings developed a strong bond, relying on each other for support and love. They found comfort and joy in performing together, showcasing their talents on the streets and in talent shows. These early experiences not only fostered Joaquin's love for acting but also proved instrumental in developing his resilience, adaptable nature, and ability to find solace amongst chaos.

As Joaquin entered the entertainment industry, he encountered professional challenges and criticism that often derailed many aspiring actors. The pervasive issue of typecasting emerged, with industry professionals consistently offering him roles that perpetuated the image of him as a child actor. Refusing to be confined by this limitation, Joaquin actively sought out diverse and challenging roles that would allow him to showcase his range and depth as an actor. This tireless pursuit required him to prove himself time and again, challenging the industry's perception and pushing the boundaries of his own capabilities.

On a personal level, Joaquin battled with inner demons and addiction, as often happens in the lives of many in the entertainment industry. The tragic death of his older brother, River Phoenix, from a drug overdose deeply affected Joaquin and intensified his own struggles. It was a wake-up call that forced him to confront his own addiction issues and seek a path to recovery. With the support of family, friends, and professional assistance, he entered rehab and made the unwavering commitment to sobriety, a decision that would have a profound impact on both his personal life and career.

Overcoming addiction and reclaiming his personal power became a pivotal moment in Joaquin's life and career. It allowed him to regain control of his artistic trajectory and fully commit himself to honing his craft. The journey towards sobriety also instilled in him a sense of empathy and a deep understanding of the challenges faced by others in similar situations. In turn, this personal growth has influenced the depth and sincerity of his performances, as he draws from his own experiences to bring authenticity and raw emotion to his characters.

chatvariety.com

In addition to personal struggles, Joaquin has also faced professional adversity. Creative conflicts, disputes, and even controversial moments have been part of his journey. One notable incident was his 2009 appearance on the Late Show with David Letterman, where he appeared disheveled and gave a perplexing interview, later revealed to be a stunt for the mockumentary "I'm Still Here." While the incident caused confusion and garnered backlash, it showcased Joaquin's commitment to his craft and his willingness to push boundaries in pursuit of his artistic vision.

However, through open communication, compromise, and a dedication to the art, he has managed to find resolutions to conflicts and maintain strong relationships with fellow actors, directors, and industry professionals. Take, for example, his collaborative partnership with director Paul Thomas Anderson in films like "The Master" and "Inherent Vice." Not only do these collaborations showcase their shared creative vision, but they also highlight Joaquin's ability to work harmoniously within a team, respecting and inspiring his fellow artists.

By overcoming his personal challenges and adversity, Joaquin Phoenix has emerged as not only an exceptional actor but also as an inspiring figure for many. His ability to confront and triumph over personal demons serves as a testament to perseverance and a reminder that even in the face of overwhelming odds, one can rise above and achieve greatness. Joaquin's tenacity and resilience have not only shaped his own trajectory but have also brought hope and inspiration to those who resonate with his struggles.

chatvariety.com

In the next chapter, we will explore the pivotal moment of reevaluation that led Joaquin to dedicate himself fully to his craft, paving the way for his rise to fame in the film industry.

chatvariety.com

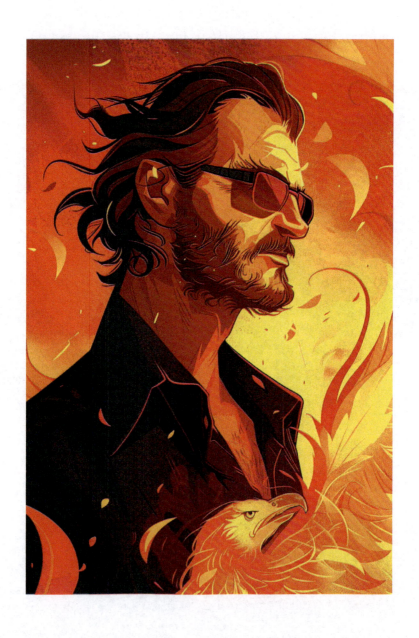

chatvariety.com

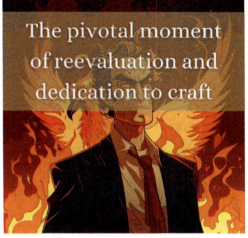

chapter 08

The pivotal moment of reevaluation and dedication to craft

Joaquin Phoenix's journey in the entertainment industry hasn't been without its challenges. After experiencing early success and acclaim, he found himself at a point of reevaluation and reflection. It was a pivotal moment in his career, one in which he questioned his choices, his motivations, and his commitment to his craft.

At this juncture, Phoenix made a conscious decision to step back and take a hard look at his career path. He recognized that he had fallen into a pattern of accepting roles that didn't challenge him creatively and that didn't align with his artistic vision. It was a moment of self-discovery and self-awareness, leading him to reevaluate his priorities and make a commitment to his craft.

With a newfound dedication to his work, Phoenix embarked on a rigorous process of self-improvement and exploration. He immersed himself in studying the great actors that came before him, delving into their techniques and methods. He became a student of his craft, constantly pushing himself to grow and evolve as an actor.

c h a t v a r i e t y . c o m

During this period, Phoenix also sought out collaborations with visionary directors who shared his passion for pushing boundaries and telling compelling stories. He actively sought out projects that allowed him to showcase his range as an actor and break free from any previous typecasting. It was a conscious effort to redefine himself and his career, and it resulted in some of his most memorable performances.

One of the significant turning points during this reevaluation phase was his work with director Paul Thomas Anderson in the critically acclaimed film "The Master." Phoenix fully embraced the character of Freddie Quell, immersing himself in the role and delivering a transformative performance. The film and his portrayal earned him widespread praise and marked a crucial shift in his career trajectory.

Phoenix's dedication to his craft extended beyond simply delivering powerful performances. He also committed himself to the process of preparing for roles. He would undergo intense physical and psychological transformations, sometimes losing or gaining significant weight, altering his appearance, and fully embodying the essence of his characters. It was a testament to his commitment and his willingness to go above and beyond for the sake of his art.

As a result of his reevaluation and dedication to his craft, Phoenix experienced a resurgence in his career. He became known for his ability to fully immerse himself in every role, bringing a raw and authentic energy to the screen. He became an actor that filmmakers and audiences alike admired and respected.

chatvariety.com

This pivotal moment of reevaluation and dedication to his craft was not without its challenges. Phoenix faced criticism and skepticism from those who questioned his commitment and doubted his ability to break away from his past roles. However, he remained steadfast in his pursuit, allowing his performances to speak for themselves and silencing any doubts.

The depth of Phoenix's commitment to his craft was also evident in his approach to character development. He would spend countless hours researching, studying, and observing real-life individuals who shared similarities with the characters he portrayed. This not only allowed him to understand their perspectives but also enabled him to bring a genuine sense of authenticity to his performances.

Furthermore, Phoenix's dedication extended beyond his individual roles. He also actively participated in the filmmaking process, immersing himself in the collaborative aspects of bringing a story to life. He would engage in conversations with directors and fellow cast members, constantly seeking to refine and enhance the narrative. His passion for storytelling was undeniable, and he became known for his insightful contributions and willingness to go the extra mile to ensure the success of each project.

Through his unwavering commitment, Joaquin Phoenix transformed himself into a true artist. His work became more than just acting; it became an exploration of the human condition, a deep dive into the complexities of emotions and character. Audiences were captivated by his ability to tap into the core of these characters, making them relatable and deeply resonant.

c h a t v a r i e t y . c o m

This chapter explores the transformative process that took place during this pivotal moment, shedding light on the challenges, triumphs, and growth that Joaquin Phoenix experienced. His dedication to his craft set him apart from his peers and solidified his place as one of the most talented and respected actors of his generation. The impact of his commitment reverberated not only through his own career but also through the film industry as a whole, inspiring others to approach their art with the same level of dedication and passion.

As Phoenix continued to delve deeper into his craft, he sought out unconventional roles that would push the boundaries of his abilities. This quest for artistic growth led him to collaborate with director Spike Jonze on the film "Her," where he portrayed a man who falls in love with an artificially intelligent operating system. Phoenix's ability to convey raw emotions in an unorthodox narrative context demonstrated his willingness to take risks and challenge societal norms.

In addition to exploring complex fictional characters, Phoenix also gravitated towards portraying real-life individuals with extraordinary stories. His portrayal of Johnny Cash in "Walk the Line" showcased his dedication in meticulously studying Cash's mannerisms, cadence, and vocal inflections. Phoenix didn't merely imitate Cash; he internalized his essence, capturing the soul of the iconic musician and earning widespread acclaim for his transformative performance.

c h a t v a r i e t y . c o m

Phoenix's commitment to his craft went beyond the requirements of any specific role. He continuously sought opportunities to expand his artistic horizons and experiment with different forms of storytelling. This drive led him to collaborate with director Lynne Ramsay on the psychological thriller "You Were Never Really Here," where he played a traumatized war veteran turned vigilante. The character's struggles with mental health required Phoenix to explore the depths of human despair, leading him to undergo a prolonged period of introspection and internal exploration to accurately convey the character's torment.

Throughout his career, Phoenix's dedication proved that greatness in the arts is not achieved by merely playing it safe. It requires a willingness to challenge oneself, constantly pushing personal boundaries, and confronting uncomfortable emotions. This commitment often had a profound impact on both Phoenix and those around him. He became known for fostering an atmosphere of creative exploration on set, encouraging his fellow actors and collaborators to think outside the box and discover new layers within themselves.

Joaquin Phoenix's pivotal moment of reevaluation and dedication to his craft served as a beacon of inspiration for aspiring artists. His unwavering commitment to authenticity and storytelling challenged societal norms and opened up new possibilities for actors and filmmakers alike. Through his transformative performances and continuous pursuit of artistic growth, Phoenix not only solidified his legacy as a distinguished actor but also left an indelible mark on the world of cinema. His story is a testament to the power of dedication and resilience in the pursuit of creative excellence.

chatvariety.com

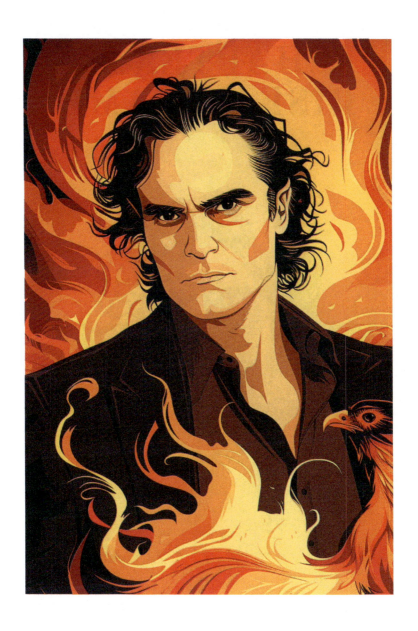

CHAPTER 3: RISE TO FAME

chatvariety.com

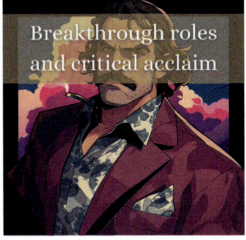

chapter 09

Breakthrough roles and critical acclaim

In this chapter, we delve into the pivotal moments in Joaquin Phoenix's career that led to his breakthrough roles and critical acclaim. As a versatile actor, Phoenix has constantly challenged himself and sought out unique opportunities to showcase his talent. From his transformative portrayal of Commodus in "Gladiator" to his award-winning performance as Joker, Phoenix has left an indelible mark on the world of cinema.

One of the defining moments in Phoenix's career came with his role as Commodus in Ridley Scott's epic film "Gladiator" (2000). This performance not only garnered him immense critical acclaim but also earned him an Academy Award nomination for Best Supporting Actor. Phoenix's portrayal of the complex and villainous character showcased his ability to bring depth and nuance to any role. He brilliantly captured Commodus' inner turmoil, embodying both his ruthlessness and fragile ego. The intensity of his performance, coupled with his skillful portrayal of the character's psychological complexities, catapulted Phoenix into the spotlight and solidified his status as a force to be reckoned with in the industry.

chatvariety.com

Following the success of "Gladiator," Phoenix continued to impress audiences and critics alike with his role as Johnny Cash in the biographical film "Walk the Line" (2005). This performance was a game-changer for Phoenix and solidified his position as one of the most talented actors of his generation. Phoenix dedicated months to preparing for the role, learning to play the guitar and sing like Cash to ensure an authentic portrayal. He immersed himself in the world of the iconic musician, delving into his troubled life, his struggles with addiction, and his tumultuous relationship with June Carter. The result was a mesmerizing performance that captured the essence of Cash, both as a musician and as a man. Phoenix's dedication to capturing the emotional and physical nuances of the character earned him widespread acclaim, including an Academy Award nomination for Best Actor and a Golden Globe win.

Further cementing his reputation for transformative performances, Phoenix took on the role of Freddie Quell in Paul Thomas Anderson's "The Master" (2012). This portrayal of a troubled World War II veteran struggling with post-traumatic stress disorder showcased Phoenix's unparalleled commitment to his craft. In preparation for the role, Phoenix engaged in extensive research, studying the psychological effects of war and delving into the depths of his character's trauma. He underwent a radical physical transformation, losing a significant amount of weight to accurately represent Freddie's mental and emotional state. The result was a raw and intense performance that left audiences captivated and moved. Phoenix's portrayal earned him numerous awards and nominations, including another Oscar nomination for Best Actor, and solidified his reputation as an actor willing to push boundaries and explore the darkest corners of the human psyche.

chatvariety.com

Phoenix's collaboration with director Spike Jonze in the film "Her" (2013) marked yet another milestone in his career. In the film, Phoenix played the lead character Theodore, who develops an emotional relationship with an artificial intelligence system. Though primarily a voice role, Phoenix masterfully conveyed Theodore's emotions, longing, and vulnerability, leaving audiences captivated by his heartfelt performance. He seamlessly portrayed the complexities of a relationship that transcended physicality, showcasing his ability to create genuine connections and evoke empathy. Phoenix's nuanced and layered portrayal demonstrated his versatility as an actor and further solidified his position as a force to be reckoned with in the industry.

Another standout role that further solidified Phoenix's reputation as an exceptional actor was his portrayal of the iconic DC Comics villain Joker in Todd Phillips' film of the same name (2019). With his intense and transformative performance, Phoenix delved into the depths of the character's psyche, unraveling the layers of trauma and isolation that shaped the Joker's identity. He immersed himself in the character's darkness, losing himself within the mind of a man descending into chaos. The result was a haunting and deeply affecting portrayal that captivated audiences and critics alike. Phoenix's commitment to exploring the inner workings of the character, combined with his unparalleled talent and dedication, earned him widespread acclaim and numerous accolades. He received his first Academy Award for Best Actor for this role, solidifying his status as a force to be reckoned with in the industry.

chatvariety.com

Throughout his career, Joaquin Phoenix has continuously pushed boundaries and taken on challenging and unconventional roles. His commitment to his craft, coupled with his remarkable talent and unwavering dedication, has resulted in a string of breakthrough performances and critical acclaim. Each role has showcased Phoenix's ability to completely immerse himself in the characters he plays, captivating audiences and leaving an indelible mark on the world of cinema. Whether it's his physical transformations, his mastery of accents and vocal intonations, or his commitment to understanding the emotional core of a character, Phoenix's performances continue to astound and inspire, solidifying his place as one of the most revered actors of his generation.

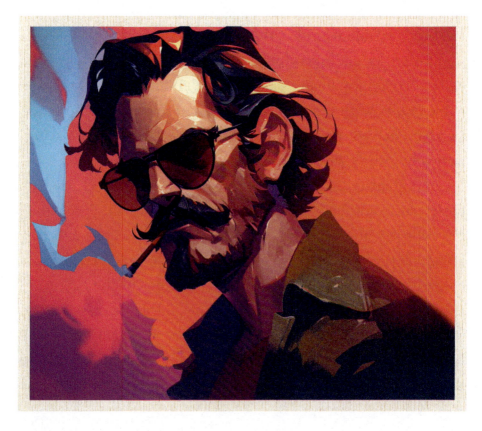

chatvariety.com

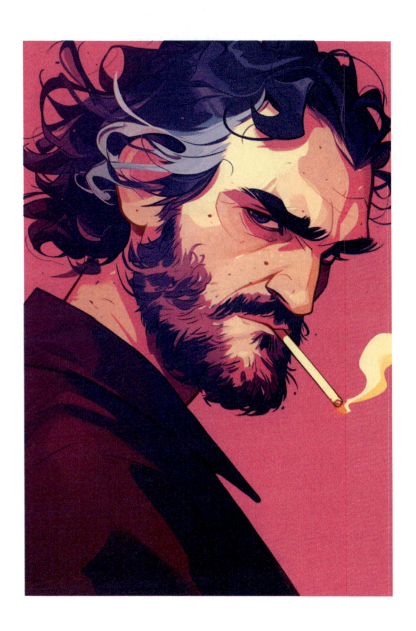

chatvariety.com

Key movies that defined his career path

Throughout his illustrious career, Joaquin Phoenix has starred in numerous films that have not only made a lasting impact on audiences but also played a crucial role in defining his career path. These key movies have showcased his exceptional talent, versatility, and dedication to his craft. Let us delve into some of these remarkable films that have left an indelible mark on Phoenix's career.

1. "Gladiator" (2000): Directed by Ridley Scott, this epic historical drama saw Phoenix portray the treacherous and power-hungry Commodus, earning him widespread critical acclaim. Phoenix delved deep into the complex psyche of Commodus, a character driven by envy, power lust, and a desperate need for validation. His portrayal was nuanced, often oscillating between moments of vulnerability and sheer ruthlessness. Phoenix's uncanny ability to bring out the layers of Commodus made him a formidable antagonist, elevating the film to new heights and solidifying his presence on the silver screen.

chatvariety.com

"Gladiator" marked a turning point in Phoenix's career. While he had already established his talent in previous roles, this film catapulted him into the spotlight, cementing his reputation as a formidable actor capable of delivering powerful performances in major productions. Phoenix's portrayal of Commodus earned him an Academy Award nomination for Best Supporting Actor, further validating his status as a force to be reckoned with.

2. "Walk the Line" (2005): In this biographical drama, Phoenix stepped into the shoes of the legendary musician Johnny Cash. His portrayal captured the essence of Cash's rebellious spirit, haunted past, and unyielding devotion to music. Phoenix underwent extensive vocal and guitar training to master Cash's distinctive sound and playing style. Through his deeply affecting performance, he allowed audiences to witness Cash's tormented journey, his struggles with addiction, and the redemptive power of love. Phoenix's dedication to embodying Cash earned him numerous awards and critical acclaim, establishing him as a force to be reckoned with in the industry.

"Walk the Line" showcased Phoenix's ability to fully immerse himself in a character, not just in terms of physicality but also in capturing the essence of their soul. The film demanded a level of authenticity that Phoenix wholeheartedly embraced, showcasing his commitment to his craft. His raw and emotionally charged performance not only paid homage to Cash's legacy but also solidified Phoenix's stature as a versatile and gifted actor. The film earned Phoenix his first Academy Award nomination for Best Actor, marking a significant milestone in his career.

chatvariety.com

3. "The Master" (2012): Collaborating with director Paul Thomas Anderson, Phoenix delivered a truly transformative performance as Freddie Quell, a WWII veteran struggling with post-traumatic stress disorder. Phoenix fully immersed himself into Quell's mind - a tortured and volatile individual caught in a web of emotional turmoil. He exhibited a physicality and intensity that was raw and unfiltered, showcasing his willingness to push the boundaries of his craft. Through Phoenix's portrayal, the audience was captivated by Quell's inner struggles and drawn into a mesmerizing exploration of identity, control, and the human condition.

"The Master" marked a significant departure for Phoenix, both in terms of the complexity of the character he portrayed and the depth of the story being told. The film delved into the psychological complexities of human existence and the power dynamics that shape our lives. Phoenix's commitment to portraying Quell's volatility and vulnerability with striking authenticity garnered critical acclaim and earned him multiple awards, including the Volpi Cup for Best Actor at the Venice Film Festival. "The Master" solidified Phoenix's status as an actor unafraid to tackle challenging and intellectually stimulating projects.

chatvariety.com

4. "Her" (2013): In this futuristic romance directed by Spike Jonze, Phoenix portrayed Theodore Twombly, a lonely man who falls in love with an artificial intelligence operating system. Phoenix's performance was a delicate dance between loneliness and longing, as he conveyed the complexities of navigating love in a technologically-driven world. His ability to connect with an invisible presence and communicate genuine emotion showcased his remarkable range as an actor. Phoenix's portrayal of Theodore was simultaneously heartbreaking and hopeful, shining a light on the human capacity for connection and the yearning for meaningful relationships.

"Her" showcased a different side of Phoenix's talent. With the character of Theodore, he had to rely heavily on his emotional depth and ability to convey profound emotions without the aid of physical interactions. Phoenix accomplished this with finesse, masterfully portraying the complexities of a vulnerable and heartfelt individual seeking connection in a rapidly evolving world. His performance earned critical acclaim, with Phoenix receiving his fourth Academy Award nomination for Best Actor.

5. "Joker" (2019): Perhaps one of Phoenix's most iconic roles to date, his portrayal of the titular character in "Joker" was a tour de force performance that left audiences in awe. Phoenix fearlessly delved into the darkest corners of Arthur Fleck's mind, immersing himself in the role with unwavering commitment. Through his physically transformative appearance, haunting laughter, and nuanced portrayal, Phoenix captured the descent into madness and the bleak reality of a marginalized character. His performance was a profound exploration of the effects of society's neglect and the power of empathy, leaving a lasting impact on audiences worldwide.

chatvariety.com

"Joker" pushed the boundaries of comic book adaptations and solidified Phoenix's ability to breathe new life into iconic characters. The film was a haunting character study, with Phoenix's portrayal of Arthur Fleck delving deep into the psychological underpinnings of a man teetering on the edge of sanity. His performance was met with critical praise and accolades, earning him his first Academy Award for Best Actor. Phoenix's dedication to capturing the complexity of the character, his physical transformation, and his sheer intensity made his portrayal of Joker one of the most iconic in cinematic history.

These are just a few examples of the key movies that have defined Joaquin Phoenix's career path. Each film has showcased his immense range, emotional depth, and dedication to realizing complex characters on screen. Phoenix's choice of roles and his exceptional performances in these films have solidified his status as one of the finest actors of his generation, leaving a profound impact on the world of cinema. As he continues to take on challenging and groundbreaking projects, the trajectory of Phoenix's career promises to be filled with many more unforgettable roles and contributions to the art of filmmaking.

c h a t v a r i e t y . c o m

chatvariety.com

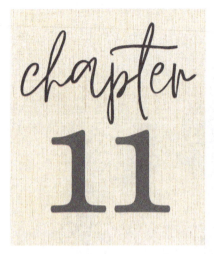

chapter 11

Behind-the-scenes insights into his rise

Joaquin Phoenix's rise to fame has been marked by a combination of talent, perseverance, and a strong work ethic. Behind the glamour and success lies a story of dedication, hard work, and strategic decision-making.

In this chapter, we delve deeper into the behind-the-scenes insights into Joaquin Phoenix's rise in the film industry. From auditions to rehearsals, from script analysis to character development, we uncover the fascinating process behind his success.

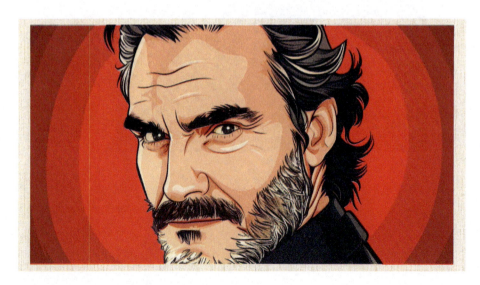

chatvariety.com

One key aspect of Phoenix's approach is his unwavering commitment to fully immersing himself in a role. He is known for his method acting techniques, often spending months meticulously researching and preparing for a character. Whether it's losing weight for "The Master" or adopting the mannerisms and voice of the Joker, Phoenix delves deep into the psyche of his characters. He tirelessly examines their motivations, their past traumas, and their relationships, allowing him to bring a profound understanding to their complexities on-screen. His dedication is unparalleled as he delves into the depths of his characters' emotional and psychological layers. Benefiting from his extensive preparation, he brings authenticity and credibility to his performances that captivate audiences globally.

Collaboration plays a pivotal role in Phoenix's journey as well. He has deliberately sought out opportunities to work with some of the most accomplished directors and seasoned actors in the industry. Through these collaborations, he has had the privilege of learning from and being inspired by the best. From his early work with legendary director Gus Van Sant in "To Die For" to his recent collaboration with Todd Phillips in "Joker," Phoenix actively seeks out chances to explore different acting techniques and varying approaches to storytelling. By immersing himself in these collaborations, he not only gains valuable insights but also builds a network of creative individuals who challenge and motivate him to push the boundaries of his craft.

chatvariety.com

A distinct aspect of Phoenix's rise lies in his meticulous selection of projects that challenge him and offer unique opportunities for growth. Unwilling to succumb to complacency or typecasting, he has consistently demonstrated the courage to step out of his comfort zone and take on unconventional, thought-provoking characters. By fearlessly pushing boundaries and embracing complexity, he has garnered critical acclaim and built a reputation for choosing roles that resonate deeply with audiences. From his portrayal of Johnny Cash in "Walk the Line" to his transformative performance as the reclusive Theodore in "Her," Phoenix consistently delivers nuanced and emotionally charged performances that leave a lasting impact on audiences.

Furthermore, Phoenix's success can be attributed to his ability to adapt seamlessly to the ever-evolving landscape of the film industry. He recognizes the need to navigate between independent films and mainstream blockbusters in order to maintain his artistic integrity yet reach a broad audience. With his name attached to a project, Phoenix elevates the material, simultaneously drawing audiences to independent films and bringing nuanced performances to major studio productions. His versatility and willingness to embrace diverse projects have established him as a dynamic force in the industry.

c h a t v a r i e t y . c o m

Throughout this chapter, we are granted privileged access to a collection of firsthand accounts from the directors, producers, and fellow actors fortunate enough to work with Joaquin Phoenix. Their testimonials provide invaluable insight into his unwavering dedication to his craft and unwavering professionalism on set. His work ethic, preparation, and ability to tap into the essence of a character consistently earn him the respect and admiration of his peers. Through these anecdotes and stories, we gain an intimate understanding of the behind-the-scenes world of a rising star.

By the conclusion of this extended chapter, readers are provided with a profound understanding of the secret ingredients that propelled Joaquin Phoenix to his level of commendable success. It is through his relentless commitment to his art, his appreciation for collaboration, his willingness to take artistic risks, and his ability to adapt to the ever-changing industry that he has become one of the most respected and admired actors of his generation. Phoenix's indomitable spirit and passion for storytelling continue to shape his trajectory, captivating audiences worldwide and solidifying his legacy as a true master of his craft.

c h a t v a r i e t y . c o m

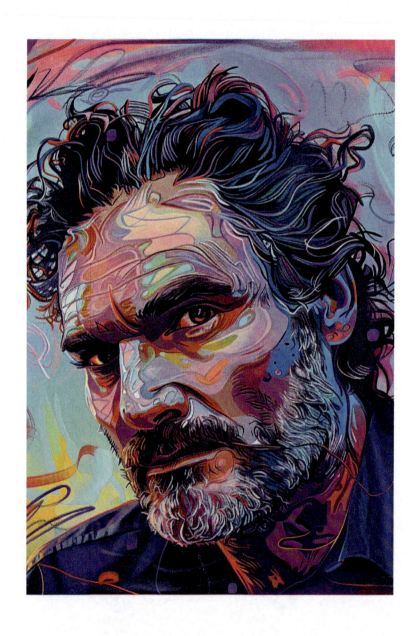

chatvariety.com

CHAPTER 4: ICONIC ROLES AND PERFORMANCES

chatvariety.com

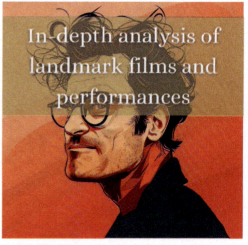

chapter 12

In-depth analysis of landmark films and performances

In this chapter, we delve into the key landmark films and performances that have shaped Joaquin Phoenix's career and solidified his status as a remarkable actor. From his early breakout roles to his more recent critically acclaimed performances, each film has showcased Phoenix's range, versatility, and commitment to his craft.

One of Phoenix's most notable roles came early in his career with the film "Gladiator" (2000), directed by Ridley Scott. In this epic historical drama, Phoenix starred as Commodus, the power-hungry and psychologically complex antagonist to Russell Crowe's protagonist, Maximus. Phoenix's portrayal of Commodus earned him widespread recognition and praise for his ability to embody such a morally ambiguous and disturbed character. His intense and captivating performance brought a menacing presence to the screen, highlighting the depths of his talent. His portrayal of Commodus was filled with a seething combination of arrogance, vulnerability, and an insatiable thirst for power. Phoenix's ability to navigate and personify the complex psyche of this character impressed both critics and audiences alike. As a result, he received his first Academy Award nomination for Best Supporting Actor, solidifying his status as a rising star in Hollywood.

chatvariety.com

Following his success in "Gladiator," Phoenix continued to impress audiences with his ability to immerse himself in a wide range of characters. In the romantic drama "Her" (2013), directed by Spike Jonze, Phoenix portrayed Theodore Twombly, a lonely man who develops a deep emotional connection with an artificial intelligence operating system. Unlike other romantic films, "Her" explores the complexities of human emotions and the impact of technology on relationships. Phoenix's performance was praised for its sensitivity and vulnerability, allowing audiences to empathize with Theodore's complex emotional journey. His portrayal was nuanced, capturing the essence of a man yearning for connection in a deeply introspective and heartfelt manner. Phoenix skillfully blended the joy and pain of Theodore's experiences, creating a character that felt achingly real. His ability to effectively convey emotions alongside an operating system showcased his versatility as an actor and his mastery of subtlety. "Her" became another significant film in Phoenix's career, showcasing his ability to captivate audiences with his authentic and emotive performances.

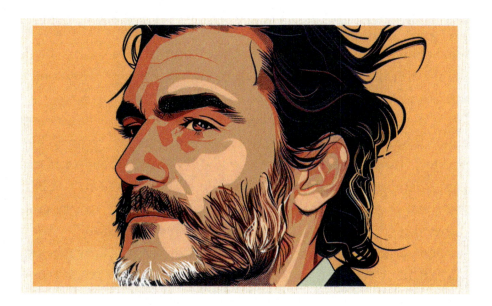

chatvariety.com

Another monumental performance in Phoenix's career came in the form of his portrayal of Johnny Cash in the biographical drama "Walk the Line" (2005). Directed by James Mangold, the film depicted the life and struggles of the legendary musician. Phoenix not only mastered Cash's distinctive vocal style but also captured the essence of his persona, showcasing both his vulnerabilities and his rebellious spirit. Phoenix's performance went beyond mere impersonation, delving into the emotional depths of Johnny Cash, and portraying his complexities with a raw intensity that mesmerized audiences. His remarkable transformation and dedication to the role were evident in every scene, as he imbued the character with a combination of charisma, pain, and musical talent. Phoenix's ability to convey Cash's inner turmoil, passion, and artistry earned him numerous accolades, including the Golden Globe for Best Actor and an Academy Award nomination for Best Actor. "Walk the Line" solidified Phoenix's standing as one of the most talented actors of his generation.

Taking on the challenging role of Freddie Quell in Paul Thomas Anderson's "The Master" (2012), Phoenix once again showcased his ability to fully immerse himself in complex characters. The film revolves around the relationship between Quell, a troubled naval veteran, and Lancaster Dodd, played by Philip Seymour Hoffman. Phoenix's performance as Freddie Quell was a tour de force, marked by his commitment to capturing the character's inner demons and struggles. He underwent a remarkable physical transformation and infused Freddie Quell with an unpredictable energy that kept audiences captivated. Phoenix's portrayal was characterized by a unique blend of volatility and vulnerability, exposing the layers of trauma and instability that defined Freddie Quell. His raw intensity and unwavering commitment resulted in a mesmerizing performance, earning him his third Academy Award nomination for Best Actor.

c h a t v a r i e t y . c o m

One of Phoenix's most iconic performances came in the form of playing the titular character in "Joker" (2019), directed by Todd Phillips. This psychological thriller explores the origins of the infamous Batman villain, delving into the descent of Arthur Fleck into madness. Phoenix's portrayal of Fleck was a revelation, as he fearlessly treaded into darkness, creating a haunting, layered, and deeply unhinged character. His transformative physicality, emotional depth, and dedication to the role made his performance unforgettable, elevating the film into a cinematic masterpiece. Phoenix captivated audiences with his ability to humanize the villain and portray his struggles with mental illness and societal indifference. His portrayal was marked by an unsettling blend of vulnerability, rage, and haunting laughter, showcasing the depths of Arthur Fleck's descent into darkness. Phoenix's captivating performance gained universal acclaim, earning him numerous accolades, including the Academy Award for Best Actor. "Joker" solidified Phoenix's status as one of the greatest actors of his generation, with his portrayal destined to be remembered as one of the most iconic in film history.

Throughout his career, Joaquin Phoenix has continuously chosen roles that challenge and push the boundaries of his abilities. His dedication to fully inhabiting his characters, combined with his intense performances, has solidified his status as one of the most respected and sought-after actors in Hollywood. Each landmark film discussed in this chapter not only showcases Phoenix's acting prowess but also highlights his ability to bring depth and humanity to every role he undertakes.

chatvariety.com

Beyond his acclaimed filmography, Phoenix is known for his involvement in meaningful and thought-provoking projects. In 2018, he starred as Joe in "You Were Never Really Here," directed by Lynne Ramsay. This thriller follows the story of a traumatized veteran turned hitman, showcasing Phoenix's ability to delve into the darkest depths of the human psyche. His performance captivated audiences and critics alike, earning him the Best Actor award at the Cannes Film Festival. Phoenix's portrayal of Joe was an exercise in restraint and intensity, as he effectively conveyed the character's trauma, compassion, and vigilante drive. His commitment to representing the complexity of Joe's character without relying on conventional dialogue was a testament to his skill as an actor.

Furthermore, Phoenix's dedication to his craft extends beyond just delivering exceptional performances on screen. He is also known for his commitment to raising awareness about important social and environmental issues. In 2020, during his acceptance speech at the Academy Awards for his role in "Joker," Phoenix passionately addressed topics such as climate change, animal rights, and inequality. His heartfelt words resonated with many, highlighting his genuine desire to use his platform to promote positive change. Phoenix's advocacy work and his willingness to use his fame to shed light on pressing issues have made him an influential figure in the entertainment industry.

chatvariety.com

In conclusion, Joaquin Phoenix's career is marked by a series of landmark films and performances that showcase his immense talent and dedication. From his early breakout role in "Gladiator" to his transformative portrayal of the Joker, each film demonstrates Phoenix's versatility and ability to immerse himself in complex characters. His relentless commitment to his craft, combined with his willingness to tackle meaningful projects, has solidified his status as a remarkable actor and a prominent advocate for social and environmental issues. Phoenix's impacton the film industry is undeniable, as he continues to push boundaries and challenge the norms of storytelling. His performances have captivated audiences and critics alike, earning him numerous awards and nominations, including three Academy Award nominations and one win.

What sets Phoenix apart from many other actors is his ability to fully embody his characters, to the point where it feels like he disappears into them. His physicality, mannerisms, and even his voice undergo dramatic transformations to suit the roles he takes on. Whether it's bulking up for his role as the villainous Commodus in "Gladiator" or losing a significant amount of weight to portray the emaciated Arthur Fleck in "Joker," Phoenix's commitment to accurately portraying his characters is truly commendable.

Beyond his physical transformations, Phoenix also delves deep into the emotional and psychological aspects of his characters. He approaches each role with meticulous preparation and research, spending months immersing himself in their world and understanding their motivations. His performances are characterized by a raw intensity and an ability to tap into the depth of human emotions. Phoenix isn't afraid to explore the darker, grittier aspects of humanity, and his willingness to push boundaries and take risks is what sets him apart.

chatvariety.com

In addition to his exceptional acting skills, Phoenix also has a keen eye for choosing meaningful and thought-provoking scripts. He is drawn to stories that delve into complex and challenging themes, such as mental illness, loneliness, and societal issues. Through his performances, he creates a deep connection with audiences, allowing them to reflect on these topics and generate conversation.

Moreover, Phoenix's commitment to using his fame for positive change is inspiring. He is an outspoken advocate for social and environmental issues, using his platform to raise awareness and call for action. Whether it's speaking about animal rights, climate change, or inequality, Phoenix's passion and authenticity shine through. His actions align with his beliefs, as he lives a vegan lifestyle and actively supports organizations and initiatives that work towards creating a more sustainable and compassionate world.

In conclusion, Joaquin Phoenix's career is marked by groundbreaking films and performances that showcase his immense talent, commitment, and versatility as an actor. From his early breakout role in "Gladiator" to his transformative portrayal of the Joker, Phoenix consistently delivers captivating performances that leave a lasting impact on audiences. His dedication to his craft, his willingness to tackle challenging and thought-provoking roles, and his advocacy work make him a true force in the film industry. Joaquin Phoenix has undoubtedly left an indelible mark on cinema, and his legacy will continue to inspire and influence future generations of actors.

c h a t v a r i e t y . c o m

chatvariety.com

chapter 13

Method acting: preparation and process for major roles

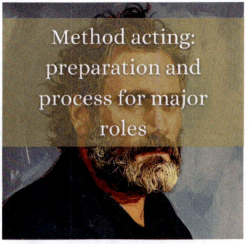

Joaquin Phoenix is renowned for his dedication to his craft and his commitment to portraying characters with depth and authenticity. One of the key aspects of his approach to acting is his utilization of the method acting technique. Method acting involves immersing oneself fully in the character's emotions, experiences, and thoughts, often blurring the line between the actor's own identity and that of the character they are portraying.

For each major role, Phoenix embarks on an intensive process of research and preparation to fully understand and embody the character he will be portraying. This typically involves extensive reading, studying real-life individuals or circumstances related to the character, and delving into their emotional core.

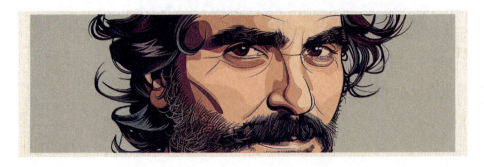

chatvariety.com

Phoenix takes great care in understanding the historical, sociological, and psychological context of his characters. He goes beyond the script, diving into books, articles, and documentaries that offer insights into the character's background, motivations, and environment. By immersing himself in these resources, Phoenix gains a clearer understanding of the character's mindset and can develop a more nuanced and authentic portrayal.

Furthermore, Phoenix often engages in physical transformations to enhance his portrayal. He alters his appearance through weight gain or loss, changes hairstyles, and sometimes even adopts accents or specific body language to fully inhabit the character. These transformations not only impact his physical appearance but also influence his mindset, allowing him to step into the character's shoes more convincingly.

Physical transformations play a significant role in how Phoenix connects with his characters. He approaches these changes with a meticulous and disciplined mindset. For example, in preparation for his role in "Joker," Phoenix lost a considerable amount of weight to convey the character's emaciated physique. This transformation required him to adapt his diet and engage in a rigorous exercise regimen that impacted not only his body but also his mental and emotional state. By experiencing physical changes alongside his character, Phoenix deepens his understanding of their struggles and challenges.

c h a t v a r i e t y . c o m

To fully inhabit a character, Phoenix goes beyond the surface level. He delves into their emotional world, seeking to comprehend their joys, fears, and vulnerabilities. This involves researching mental and emotional experiences related to the character, consulting with experts in the field, and connecting with individuals who have similar life experiences. By immersing himself in these emotional depths, Phoenix can tap into the character's psyche and bring forth a more genuine and resonant performance.

Furthermore, being in character is not limited to the time spent on set. Phoenix carries the essence of his characters with him off-camera as well. This continuous state of immersion allows him to maintain a deep connection to the character's mindset and emotions, enabling a seamless transition between his personal and professional lives. This commitment often extends beyond the duration of the film, as Phoenix finds himself reflecting on and processing the character's experiences long after the project is complete.

Remaining in character during the filming process helps Phoenix maintain the emotional truth of the character's journey. By staying connected to the character's mindset, he is able to tap into the emotions and experiences required for each scene, allowing for a genuine response and authentic interactions with other actors. This approach infuses his performances with an unparalleled depth and realism that resonates with audiences.

chatvariety.com

Phoenix's commitment to method acting can be seen in various roles throughout his career. For example, his portrayal of Johnny Cash in "Walk the Line" involved intensive vocal training to mimic Cash's singing style, as well as learning to play guitar. His portrayal of Arthur Fleck in "Joker" included researching mental illness, losing a significant amount of weight, and practicing the character's distinctive laugh to bring a sense of realism and authenticity to the role.

The method acting approach not only allows Phoenix to create compelling and realistic performances, but it also helps him to connect with the emotions and experiences of the characters on a deep level. By fully immersing himself in their world, he is able to bring a sense of truth and vulnerability to his portrayals that resonates with audiences.

Despite the intensity of his method acting process, Phoenix is mindful of the toll it can take on his mental and emotional well-being. He emphasizes the importance of self-care and surrounding himself with a supportive team during the filming process to ensure a healthy balance between the character and his own identity.

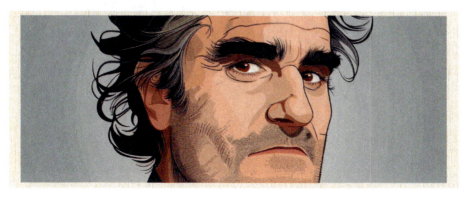

chatvariety.com

In conclusion, Chapter 13 explores Joaquin Phoenix's method of preparation and process for major roles. His dedication to extensive research, physical transformation, and immersion in the character's mindset are integral to his approach. Phoenix's commitment to authenticity and willingness to blur the boundaries between himself and the characters he portrays contribute to the incredible depth and power of his performances. His method acting technique allows him to create nuanced and compelling portrayals that resonate with audiences, showcasing his unparalleled talent as an actor.

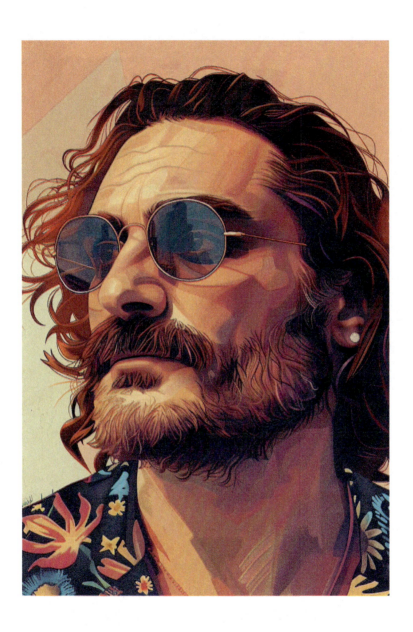

chatvariety.com

chapter 14

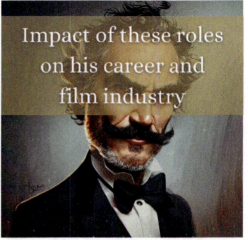

Impact of these roles on his career and film industry

Joaquin Phoenix's career has been defined by his exceptional talent and commitment to his roles, leaving a profound impact on both his trajectory as an actor and the film industry as a whole. His performances have not only captivated audiences but also challenged the boundaries of cinema and inspired a new generation of artists.

One of the defining aspects of Phoenix's impact is his ability to completely inhabit his characters, infusing them with authenticity and depth. His portrayal of Johnny Cash in "Walk the Line" was a transformative experience for the actor, and it resonated deeply with audiences. Phoenix delved into Cash's tumultuous life, mastering the art of singing and playing the guitar, and embodying the soul of the legendary musician. The result was a stunning performance that earned him critical acclaim, an Academy Award nomination, and secured his status as a force to be reckoned with in the industry.

chatvariety.com

Phoenix's magnetic presence on-screen is not limited to biopics; he has demonstrated his versatility and willingness to take risks throughout his career. In Todd Phillips' "Joker," Phoenix delivered a haunting portrayal of a troubled loner descending into madness. With his commitment to the role, he transformed physically and emotionally, fully embodying the character's pain, vulnerability, and sinister nature. This portrayal not only earned him an Academy Award but also sparked conversations surrounding mental health and society, pushing the boundaries of what a superhero film could be.

Beyond his own personal achievements, Phoenix's collaborations with visionary directors have reshaped storytelling and filmmaking. In Paul Thomas Anderson's "The Master," he mesmerized audiences as Freddie Quell, a deeply troubled alcoholic World War II veteran. The film explored themes of faith, manipulation, and the search for purpose in life, showcasing Phoenix's remarkable ability to convey raw emotion and complex character dynamics. His performance earned him widespread critical acclaim and a nomination for the Academy Award for Best Actor.

In Spike Jonze's "Her," Phoenix played Theodore Twombly, a man who falls in love with an artificial intelligence operating system. The film delved into the complexities of human connection, loneliness, and the blurred lines between the virtual and the real. Phoenix's subtle and nuanced performance anchored the film in authenticity, leading to widespread praise and another Academy Award nomination.

chatvariety.com

Notably, Phoenix's impact extends beyond the realms of critical acclaim and awards recognition. His performances have consistently resonated with audiences, translating into commercial success for many of his films. From the Oscar-winning "Gladiator," where he played the malevolent Commodus, to the critically acclaimed "Inherent Vice" and "You Were Never Really Here," Phoenix consistently delivers performances that resonate with audiences and contribute to the profitability of the film industry. This influence at the box office further solidifies Phoenix's status as one of the most sought-after actors in the industry, forming a symbiotic relationship between his artistic integrity and commercial viability.

Furthermore, Phoenix's commitment to his craft and dedication to portraying complex characters have ignited inspiration among fellow actors. His fearless approach to challenging roles has set a new standard for authenticity and dedication in the industry. Many actors look to Phoenix as an inspiration, seeing him as a trailblazer who fearlessly explores the depths of human emotion, compelling others to push their own boundaries in pursuit of mastery in their respective crafts.

As an industry innovator, Joaquin Phoenix has redefined the possibilities of storytelling by daringly venturing into unconventional territories. His roles showcase a unique blend of vulnerability, intensity, and emotional resonance, leaving a profound impact on audiences and industry peers alike. By fearlessly embodying a diverse range of complex characters, Phoenix's performances have spurred conversations around social issues, mental health, and the human condition, elevating the art of film to new heights.

chatvariety.com

In conclusion, Joaquin Phoenix's roles have left an indelible mark on his career and the film industry at large. His ability to fully inhabit his characters, his groundbreaking collaborations, and his impact on the box office illustrate his profound influence. Phoenix's talent, dedication, and willingness to take risks have solidified his place as an icon of contemporary cinema, leaving a lasting legacy that promises to continue inspiring future generations of actors and filmmakers.

chatvariety.com

CHAPTER 5: THE CRAFT OF TRANSFORMATION

chatvariety.com

chapter 15

Exploration of his unique approach to character building

Joaquin Phoenix is renowned for his ability to fully immerse himself in the characters he portrays. In this chapter, we delve into his unique approach to character building, which sets him apart from other actors in the industry.

One aspect that sets Phoenix apart is his dedication to extensive research. His commitment to fully understanding the backgrounds and experiences of his characters is second to none. Whether it's studying real-life individuals, reading books, studying historical events, or talking to experts in the field, Phoenix goes to great lengths to gather a wealth of knowledge that will inform his performances. This deep research allows him to ground his characters in reality and provides him with a solid foundation to draw from during his preparations and on-set improvisations.

chatvariety.com

Furthermore, Phoenix is known for his deeply internal process of character development. He not only focuses on understanding the external traits of a character but delves into their psychological makeup as well. He asks probing questions about their motivations, desires, and fears, creating a rich inner life for his characters. This deep understanding of his characters' mindset allows him to authentically portray their emotions, struggles, and growth throughout the narrative arc. By tapping into the intricacies of their psychology, he engenders empathy and genuine connection between the character and the audience.

Phoenix's attention to detail also extends to the physicality and mannerisms of his characters. He meticulously studies body language, gestures, and vocal nuances, understanding that these elements play a critical role in bringing a character to life. He observes real people, including those who share similarities with his character's background or profession, to capture the subtlest of mannerisms. He often records his own movements, practicing them until they become second nature, allowing him to seamlessly embody his characters, even in their physicality. This level of dedication to the physical presence of a character adds another layer of authenticity to his performances, making them feel fully realized.

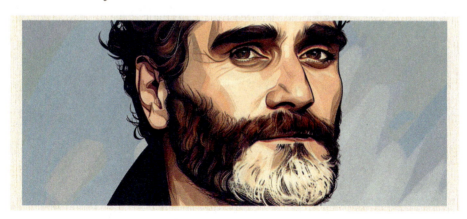

c h a t v a r i e t y . c o m

In addition to these methods, Phoenix also prioritizes emotional authenticity in his performances. He believes in channeling his own emotions and experiences into his characters, allowing himself to fully feel and embody the emotions his characters would experience. By drawing from his own emotional well, he brings an unparalleled depth and vulnerability to his characters, making their experiences feel vivid and genuine. This approach requires a delicate balance between personal connection and maintaining the integrity of the character's unique emotional journey, a skill Phoenix has refined over his illustrious career.

It is worth noting that Phoenix's approach to character building is not confined to a specific method or technique. He draws inspiration from various acting schools, including Meisner, Method, and Stanislavski, and adapts them to suit the specific demands of each role. This versatility showcases his versatility as an actor and allows him to bring a diverse range of characters to life with depth and conviction. His ability to seamlessly merge these techniques based on the needs of a character is testament to his artistic intuition and his dedication to presenting the most truthful and multi-dimensional performances.

chatvariety.com

Another fascinating aspect of Phoenix's approach is his willingness to take risks and push boundaries. He actively seeks out roles that challenge societal norms and conventions, both physically and emotionally. He is not afraid to engage in physically and emotionally demanding roles that require intense transformation, often undergoing significant physical changes to better embody his characters. In films like "Joker," where he shed weight and altered his physique to represent the decayed state of his character, his dedication to the role was palpable. This fearlessness in embracing demanding roles allows him to explore the depths of human experience and tackle complex and challenging characters, leaving an indelible mark on the audience.

The result of Phoenix's unique approach to character building is an extraordinary ability to transform himself completely. From his physical appearance to his internal state, Phoenix has the capacity to become someone entirely different from himself. His dedication to thorough research, psychological exploration, physical transformation, emotional authenticity, and a willingness to take risks all coalesce to create performances that are truly captivating and unforgettable.

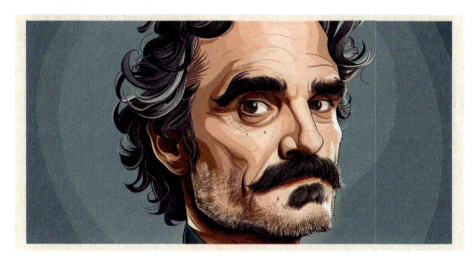

c h a t v a r i e t y . c o m

In conclusion, Joaquin Phoenix's approach to character building is a multifaceted process that encompasses extensive research, psychological exploration, physical transformation, emotional authenticity, and a willingness to take risks. This unique approach sets him apart as one of the most talented and captivating actors of our time. Through his meticulous preparation and unwavering dedication, Phoenix consistently delivers performances that resonate with audiences on a profound level, leaving a lasting impact on the world of cinema. His ability to embody the essence of his characters, both externally and internally, ensures that his performances are authentic, compelling, and deeply memorable.

chatvariety.com

chatvariety.com

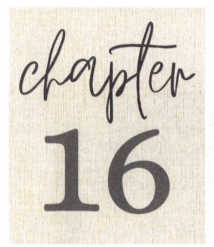
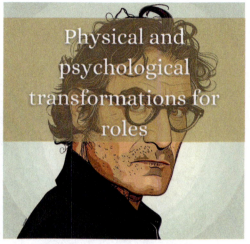

Chapter 16: Physical and psychological transformations for roles

In his illustrious career, Joaquin Phoenix has become renowned for his ability to completely immerse himself in his roles. One of the key aspects of his approach is his dedication to physical and psychological transformations for each character he portrays.

When it comes to physical transformations, Phoenix has demonstrated an astounding commitment to altering his appearance to suit the needs of his roles. He understands that a character's physicality plays a crucial role in telling their story and capturing their essence. Whether it is losing or gaining weight, changing his hairstyle, or even modifying his posture and mannerisms, Phoenix goes to great lengths to ensure that he physically embodies the essence of his characters.

chatvariety.com

For his role as Johnny Cash in "Walk the Line," Phoenix knew that merely replicating Cash's appearance wouldn't suffice. He wanted to go beyond imitation and truly capture the essence of the man. To accomplish this, Phoenix underwent a rigorous training regimen to convincingly portray the legendary musician. He learned to play the guitar and sing in Cash's unique style, effectively capturing both his voice and stage presence. Additionally, Phoenix adopted Cash's walk, stance, and mannerisms, further enhancing his transformation into the iconic figure. By immersing himself in Cash's music and history, Phoenix was able to authentically portray the complexities and struggles of the legendary musician, earning him critical acclaim and an Academy Award nomination.

In "The Master," Phoenix's portrayal of Freddie Quell required him to embody a disturbed and volatile individual. To achieve this, he delved into physical contortions, twisting and slouching his body to convey Freddie's internal turmoil. His disheveled appearance and wild eyes added to the character's sense of instability, leaving audiences both amazed and disturbed by his commitment. Phoenix understood that physicality could serve as a powerful tool to communicate the psychological state of a character, and he used it to his advantage to deliver an unforgettable performance. The intensity of his portrayal earned him numerous accolades, including a nomination for Best Actor at the Academy Awards.

c h a t v a r i e t y . c o m

Phoenix's physical transformations are often accompanied by intense psychological preparations. He understands the importance of immersing himself in the emotional and mental world of his characters, seeking to understand their motivations and insecurities. By diving deep into their psyche, Phoenix is able to shed light on the complexities that make them truly human, resulting in authentic and compelling performances that resonate with audiences.

To prepare for his role as Arthur Fleck in "Joker," Phoenix knew he needed to get inside the mind of a troubled and mentally ill individual. He devoted himself to studying the effects of isolation, trauma, and societal neglect on the human psyche, consulting with psychologists and diving into research. This deep understanding allowed him to authentically portray the character's descent into madness, capturing the vulnerability and rage that lay beneath the surface. Phoenix's physical transformation for the role, including losing a significant amount of weight and adopting a gaunt appearance, added to the unsettling portrayal of the character. By pushing himself to the limits physically and mentally, Phoenix captured the inner turmoil and vulnerability of Arthur Fleck, leaving a lasting impact on audiences worldwide. His stunning performance earned him numerous awards, including the prestigious Best Actor Oscar.

c h a t v a r i e t y . c o m

It is through these physical and psychological transformations that Joaquin Phoenix brings his characters to life on the screen. His meticulous attention to detail and willingness to push himself to the limits have become hallmarks of his craft. By completely embodying his roles, Phoenix captivates audiences, leaving them in awe of his ability to transform into the most diverse and complex characters. His commitment to physical and psychological authenticity elevates his performances, resulting in a cinematic experience that resonates long after the credits roll.

In conclusion, Chapter 16 delves into Joaquin Phoenix's dedication to physical and psychological transformations for his roles, exploring how he brings his characters to life on the screen. Through his commitment to altering his appearance and delving into the psyche of his characters, Phoenix has astounded audiences with his authenticity and ability to transcend mere imitation. His approach ensures that each performance is a fully realized portrayal, immersing viewers in the world of the film and leaving a lasting impact. From his embodiment of Johnny Cash to his transformation into the unpredictable Joker, Phoenix's dedication to physical and psychological authenticity marks him as one of the most compelling actors of his generation.

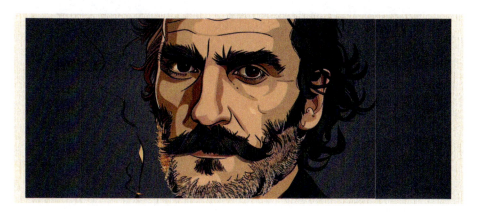

chatvariety.com

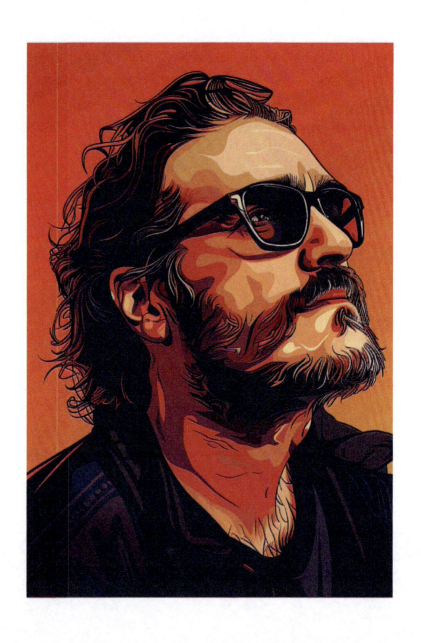

chatvariety.com

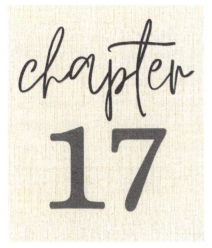
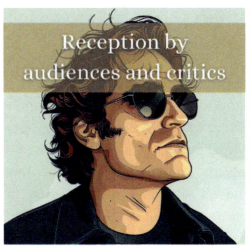

Reception by audiences and critics

chapter 17

Joaquin Phoenix's performances have consistently garnered attention and acclaim from both audiences and critics alike. With his uncanny ability to fully immerse himself in his characters and bring them to life with unparalleled authenticity, he has solidified his status as one of the most celebrated actors of his generation.

One of the aspects that sets Phoenix apart is his remarkable versatility. He effortlessly transitions between roles, effortlessly embodying characters with vastly different personalities, backgrounds, and experiences. Whether he's portraying a disturbed loner in "Joker," a compassionate lover in "Her," or a troubled musician in "Walk the Line," Phoenix's ability to captivate audiences with his nuanced portrayals is unparalleled. This versatility has allowed him to appeal to a wide range of viewers, further cementing his reputation as an actor of immense talent and depth.

chatvariety.com

Audiences have consistently responded with enthusiasm and admiration to Phoenix's work. They are often left awestruck by his commitment and dedication to his roles. His intense performances leave a lasting impact, evoking a wide range of emotions from viewers. Phoenix has the extraordinary ability to effortlessly tap into the human experience, effortlessly highlighting the intricacies of our shared emotions. It is not uncommon for audience members to find themselves deeply moved or emotionally invested in his characters. Through his work, Phoenix invites viewers to reflect on their own lives, as his characters resonate on a deeply personal level. The profound impact he leaves on audiences is a testament to his power as an actor.

Critics, too, have been vocal in their admiration of Phoenix's talent and skill. His ability to delve into the depths of his characters has earned him numerous accolades, including multiple award nominations and wins. Critics appreciate Phoenix's willingness to take on challenging and complex roles, and his transformative performances have often been hailed as some of the most astounding in recent memory. They recognize that his talent lies not only in his technical prowess but also his innate ability to convey complex emotions convincingly. Phoenix's performances are never surface-level; rather, he dares to expose the raw vulnerability and underlying truths of his characters, captivating critics and leaving them in awe of his craft.

chatvariety.com

Furthermore, Phoenix's commitment to authenticity in his performances has been widely praised. He is known for his unwavering dedication to each role, approaching every project with meticulous research and preparation. By fully immersing himself in the lives of his characters, he brings a level of truthfulness that resonates deeply with audiences and critics alike. His attention to detail, from physicality to behavioral quirks, is unmatched. By opening himself up to the emotional depths of his characters, Phoenix delivers performances that are not only technically impressive but also profoundly moving.

While the majority of responses to Phoenix's work have been overwhelmingly positive, it is important to mention that not all opinions align. Some critics have questioned his choices of roles and the intensity of his performances. They argue that his dedication to his craft sometimes borders on the extreme, leading to excessively dark and disturbing portrayals. However, it is precisely Phoenix's ability to challenge conventions and take risks that makes his work so compelling. He fearlessly explores the human condition by diving into characters that may push societal boundaries, pushing audiences and critics to confront uncomfortable truths about humanity.

chatvariety.com

In conclusion, Joaquin Phoenix's reception by both audiences and critics has been nothing short of extraordinary. His performances continue to captivate, provoke, and challenge, leaving an indelible impression on those who witness his immense talent. With each new project, anticipation for his performance reaches a crescendo, and his ability to engage and resonate with viewers remains unmatched. Joaquin Phoenix has firmly established himself as a powerhouse actor, deserving of the utmost respect and admiration. His impact on the world of cinema will undoubtedly endure for generations to come.

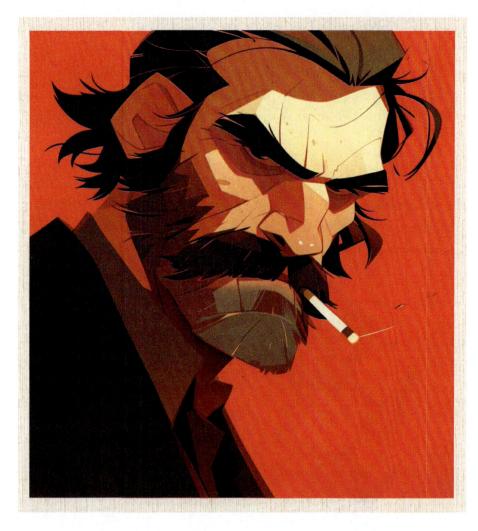

c h a t v a r i e t y . c o m

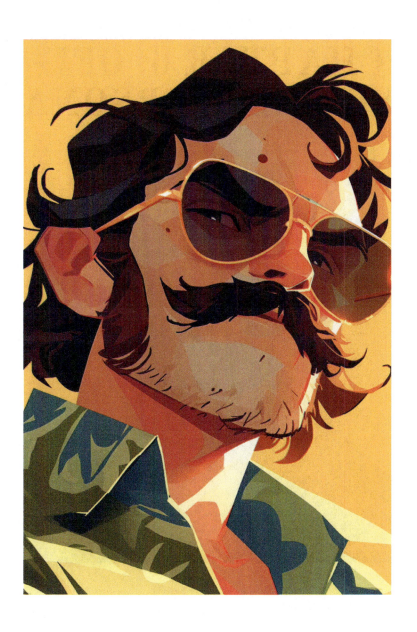

chatvariety.com

CHAPTER 6: OFF-SCREEN PERSONA

chatvariety.com

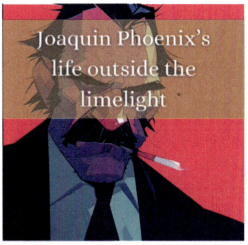

Joaquin Phoenix's life outside the limelight

In this chapter, we delve into the enigmatic and intriguing life that Joaquin Phoenix leads outside of his acting career. Unlike many celebrities who are constantly surrounded by the paparazzi and in the public eye, Phoenix is known for his low-profile lifestyle, avoiding the trappings of celebrity culture. Here, we explore the various aspects of his personal life, shedding light on his philanthropy, activism, personal beliefs, and the challenges he faces.

chatvariety.com

One noteworthy aspect of Joaquin Phoenix's life is his dedication to philanthropy. Despite his efforts to keep his personal life private, his commitment to making a positive impact on society shines through. He actively participates in several charitable organizations, often using his influence to support causes that are close to his heart. One of his most notable philanthropic endeavors is his involvement with In Defense of Animals (IDA), an organization dedicated to protecting the rights and welfare of animals. Phoenix is not only a prominent donor but also lends his voice and platform to raise awareness about the mistreatment of animals in industries such as factory farming, fur, and circuses. Through his contributions, he has helped fund rescue missions, create sanctuaries, and support legislative efforts to improve animal welfare.

In addition to his work with IDA, Phoenix has also been a longtime supporter of Rainforest Foundation, an organization focused on protecting the world's rainforests and the indigenous communities that inhabit them. He has donated substantial sums to fund efforts such as reforestation, protection of endangered species, and empowering local communities to preserve their cultural heritage. Phoenix's commitment to environmental conservation goes beyond financial support. He actively participates in campaigns and initiatives aimed at combating climate change and promoting sustainable practices. His personal life reflects these values, as he lives a sustainable lifestyle, incorporating eco-friendly choices into his daily routines.

Another aspect that distinguishes Phoenix's life outside of the limelight is his deep involvement in activism. He firmly believes that activism is not just about raising awareness but actively participating in creating change. Phoenix has been an outspoken critic of the treatment of animals, particularly in industries that profit from their exploitation. His passionate advocacy for animal rights has drawn attention to the ethical issues surrounding the meat and dairy industries, urging people to make more conscious choices and consider the impact their consumption has on the planet. Through powerful speeches and engaging interviews, Phoenix has successfully used his platform to spark important conversations and inspire others to join the fight for a more compassionate world.

In addition to his work in animal rights, Phoenix has also used his platform to raise awareness about social injustices and systemic inequalities. He has been a staunch supporter of organizations such as the American Civil Liberties Union (ACLU) and Amnesty International, lending his voice to amplify the stories of individuals affected by injustice. Phoenix's acting roles often reflect his commitment to shedding light on marginalized communities and challenging societal norms. Through his performances in films like "Joker," "The Master," and "Walk the Line," he has explored complex and flawed characters, shining a light on the complexities of the human experience and the need for empathy in an often harsh and unforgiving world.

c h a t v a r i e t y . c o m

However, the path that Phoenix has chosen is not without its challenges. His vocal stance on animal rights and other sensitive topics has often put him at odds with powerful entities and individuals deeply invested in the status quo. The actor has faced criticism and backlash from various quarters, yet he remains resolute and undeterred in his pursuit of justice and compassion. Phoenix has learned to navigate these challenges with grace and integrity, using his eloquence and fame to amplify the voices of the marginalized and create important dialogues on critical issues.

In addition to his philanthropy and activism, Phoenix's personal beliefs also play a significant role in shaping his life away from the spotlight. Known for his introspective and contemplative nature, he has embraced a more spiritual and introspective path in his journey. Phoenix has spoken openly about his exploration of mindfulness, meditation, and Eastern philosophies, which have helped him find solace, balance, and clarity in his life. These beliefs and practices have undoubtedly influenced his perspective on the world and his approach to his craft, fostering a deep sense of connection and empathy for both humans and non-human beings.

c h a t v a r i e t y . c o m

Despite his preference for privacy, Joaquin Phoenix's life outside of the limelight reveals a man driven by compassion, empathy, and a genuine desire to create positive change. His dedication to philanthropy, activism, personal beliefs, and his ability to navigate challenges exemplify his commitment to living a purposeful life beyond the confines of his acting career. Phoenix's choices and actions outside the limelight serve as an inspiration, reminding us that even those who choose to stay behind the scenes can make a profound difference in the world. Through his unwavering commitment to creating a more compassionate and just society, Joaquin Phoenix has not only transformed the lives of others but also redefined the role of celebrities in the realm of social change.

c h a t v a r i e t y . c o m

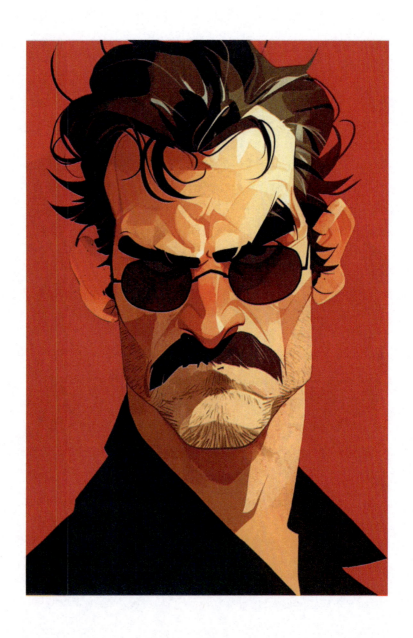

chatvariety.com

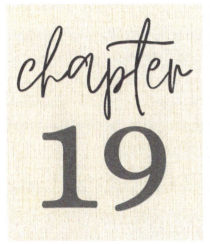

Chapter 19

Philanthropy, activism, and personal beliefs

Joaquin Phoenix is not just a talented actor; he also possesses a deep sense of social responsibility and a strong belief in using his platform for positive change. Throughout his career, he has been actively involved in various philanthropic endeavors and has used his voice to raise awareness and advocate for important causes.

One of the causes closest to Phoenix's heart is animal rights and environmental conservation. He has been a passionate vegan since a young age, deeply influenced by his family's involvement in a religious cult that emphasized compassion towards all living beings. This early upbringing sparked his commitment to align his personal beliefs with his lifestyle choices.

Phoenix's dedication to animal rights extends beyond promoting and advocating for a vegan lifestyle. He actively supports organizations like PETA (People for the Ethical Treatment of Animals), Sea Shepherd Conservation Society, and Farm Sanctuary, among others. By utilizing his fame and resources, he has been able to fund crucial campaigns that expose the cruelty of industries such as factory farming and animal testing.

Furthermore, Phoenix has been actively involved in rescue missions to save animals from abusive situations. He has personally participated in operations to shut down illegal puppy mills, rescue neglected or abandoned animals, and provide them with a second chance at life. His hands-on approach and unwavering commitment to their wellbeing have made a significant impact on the lives of numerous animals.

The documentary "Earthlings," which Phoenix narrated, serves as a stark reminder of the inhumane treatment animals endure for human consumption. This thought-provoking film explores various industries, including food, fashion, entertainment, and scientific research, to shed light on the realities of their practices. "Earthlings" has played an instrumental role in inspiring people to adopt more compassionate lifestyles and prompted them to question the ethical implications of their choices.

In addition to his work for animal rights, Phoenix has been an outspoken advocate for social justice and environmental sustainability. He has participated in protests and rallies against systemic racism, police brutality, and other injustices. In 2020, his powerful Academy Awards acceptance speech touched on a range of pressing issues, including inequality, gender equality, and climate change. With his soul-stirring words, he called for unity and encouraged individuals to reevaluate their choices and their impact on the world.

chatvariety.com

Phoenix's commitment to the environment goes far beyond rhetoric. He endeavors to live a simple and eco-friendly lifestyle, minimizing his carbon footprint and embracing sustainable practices. At his home, he uses solar panels to generate electricity, drives electric vehicles, and actively supports renewable energy initiatives. Believing in leading by example, he has invested in sustainable businesses that prioritize ethical and environmentally conscious practices.

Furthermore, Phoenix has engaged in community gardens that promote local, organic produce as an alternative to industrial agriculture. He recognizes the detrimental impact of the food industry on the environment, particularly in terms of deforestation, water pollution, and greenhouse gas emissions. By encouraging the adoption of sustainable and plant-based food alternatives, Phoenix aims to combat climate change and contribute to a more sustainable future.

Moreover, Phoenix has also engaged in humanitarian efforts, especially in supporting underprivileged communities. He has been involved in organizations like Amnesty International, supporting their work in human rights advocacy and fighting against global poverty and inequality. Recognizing the power of education as a crucial tool for empowerment, he has contributed to initiatives that aim to provide quality education to children in need. His belief in equal opportunities for all drives him to support grassroots organizations that focus on improving access to education, healthcare, and basic necessities.

c h a t v a r i e t y . c o m

Phoenix's commitment to the environment goes far beyond rhetoric. He endeavors to live a simple and eco-friendly lifestyle, minimizing his carbon footprint and embracing sustainable practices. At his home, he uses solar panels to generate electricity, drives electric vehicles, and actively supports renewable energy initiatives. Believing in leading by example, he has invested in sustainable businesses that prioritize ethical and environmentally conscious practices.

Furthermore, Phoenix has engaged in community gardens that promote local, organic produce as an alternative to industrial agriculture. He recognizes the detrimental impact of the food industry on the environment, particularly in terms of deforestation, water pollution, and greenhouse gas emissions. By encouraging the adoption of sustainable and plant-based food alternatives, Phoenix aims to combat climate change and contribute to a more sustainable future.

Moreover, Phoenix has also engaged in humanitarian efforts, especially in supporting underprivileged communities. He has been involved in organizations like Amnesty International, supporting their work in human rights advocacy and fighting against global poverty and inequality. Recognizing the power of education as a crucial tool for empowerment, he has contributed to initiatives that aim to provide quality education to children in need. His belief in equal opportunities for all drives him to support grassroots organizations that focus on improving access to education, healthcare, and basic necessities.

chatvariety.com

Phoenix's philanthropic work and activism are rooted in his genuine dedication to making a difference. He understands that his fame and influence grant him a platform to shed light on important issues and encourage others to take action. He has used his strong presence in the entertainment industry to urge the film and fashion industries to adopt sustainable practices and reduce their environmental impact. By aligning his personal beliefs with his actions, he sets an example for his fans and fellow actors alike.

In an industry often criticized for its detachment from reality, Phoenix stands out as an artist who uses his platform to challenge the status quo and advocate for a better world. Through his philanthropy, activism, and personal beliefs, he proves that true stardom goes beyond box office success; it lies in one's ability to inspire and create positive change. Joaquin Phoenix's unwavering commitment to his beliefs continues to have a profound impact, as his influential voice amplifies the calls for compassion, justice, and environmental consciousness around the globe.

c h a t v a r i e t y . c o m

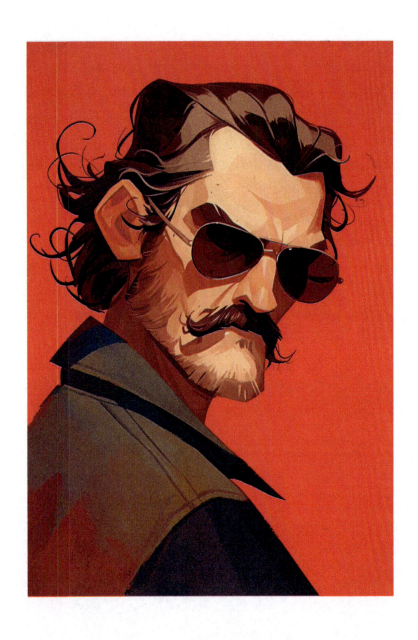

chatvariety.com

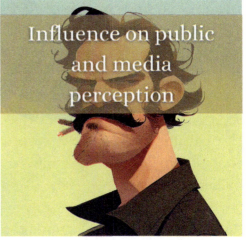

chapter 20

Influence on public and media perception

Throughout his illustrious career, Joaquin Phoenix has transcended the boundaries of traditional acting, emerging as a transformative force who delves deep into the essence of humanity. With a dedicated commitment to his craft and an unwavering pursuit of truth, Phoenix has become an indelible presence in the world of storytelling.

Phoenix's journey as an artist has been marked by a relentless pursuit of authenticity. From his early performances in Gus Van Sant's "To Die For" and Terry Gilliam's "Fear and Loathing in Las Vegas," to his more recent transformative roles in "Her" and "You Were Never Really Here," he has continually pushed the boundaries of his own abilities. It is this constant evolution and hunger for growth that sets him apart as a true artist.

In each and every role he embodies, Phoenix brings an unparalleled level of dedication and meticulous preparation. He tirelessly immerses himself in the lives and experiences of his characters, going to great lengths to understand their motivations, fears, and desires. Whether it means losing or gaining significant weight, studying accents and dialects, or training extensively to master specific skills, he leaves no stone unturned in his quest for authenticity.

chatvariety.com

This unwavering commitment to his craft extends beyond the technical aspects of acting. Phoenix believes in the power of storytelling to illuminate the human condition and spark meaningful conversations. With each performance, he digs deep into the emotional cores of his characters, crafting nuanced portrayals that resonate with audiences on a profound level. Through his art, he seeks to provoke thought, empathy, and understanding, offering a mirror to society's complexities and challenges.

One of Phoenix's defining qualities as an actor lies in his ability to bring diverse characters to life authentically. He deftly navigates the vast range of human experiences, capturing the essence of both fragile souls on the fringes of society and larger-than-life figures who leave an indelible mark on history. His embodiment of Johnny Cash in "Walk the Line" demonstrated his musical prowess and emotional depth, while his portrayal of Commodus in "Gladiator" showcased the extent of his versatility.

It is within the depths of pain and vulnerability that Phoenix finds the richest veins of truth. His most compelling performances often involve characters grappling with inner demons, haunted by past traumas, or struggling against societal expectations. In "The Master," Phoenix's portrayal of Freddie Quell exuded a raw and simmering intensity, capturing the complexities and contradictions of a man at odds with himself and the world around him.

chatvariety.com

However, it is the portrayal of Arthur Fleck in "Joker" that stands as the pinnacle of Phoenix's career thus far. This transformative performance resonated deeply with audiences worldwide, captivating them with a harrowing journey into the mind of a disturbed loner. Through his physicality and haunting presence on screen, Phoenix channeled the vulnerability and turmoil of a man pushed to the brink, exploring the dark underbelly of society's disregard for mental health and societal inequalities.

Beyond the realm of acting, Phoenix is a man of conviction, utilizing his platform to shed light on pressing global issues. He effortlessly bridges the gap between actor and activist, lending his voice to causes such as animal rights and the urgency of addressing climate change. His impassioned acceptance speech at the 92nd Academy Awards, where he called for unity and empathy, reverberated far beyond the walls of the theater, reminding us of the power of compassion in an often divided world.

Yet, even amidst the glare of the spotlight, Phoenix remains an enigmatic figure. He shies away from the trappings of fame, seeking solace in the quiet corners of his private life. This guardedness adds to the mystique that surrounds him, allowing his performances to shine brightly without the distractions of celebrity culture. It is evident that he measures his success not by the number of accolades and applause, but by the depth of the characters he brings to life and the impact his work has on the audience.

chatvariety.com

As his career continues to ascend, Joaquin Phoenix's indelible mark on the world of storytelling will undoubtedly grow. With each role, he invites us to confront our own shadows, to acknowledge our vulnerabilities, and to find solace in the collective journey towards understanding. Through his unwavering commitment to authenticity, both on and off-screen, he sets an example for aspiring artists and elevates the artistic landscape, leaving an eternal flame burning bright in the hearts of those who bear witness to his unparalleled talent.

chatvariety.com

chatvariety.com

CHAPTER 7: COLLABORATIONS AND CONTROVERSIES

chatvariety.com

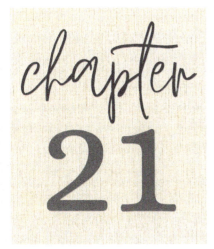

chapter 21

Key collaborations with directors and actors

Throughout his illustrious career, Joaquin Phoenix has had the incredible opportunity to collaborate with a plethora of esteemed directors and exceptional actors, resulting in some of his most extraordinary and memorable performances on the silver screen. These collaborations have not only propelled his skills as an actor to unprecedented heights but have also cemented his reputation as a versatile and intensely respected artist within the industry.

One of the most momentous collaborations in Phoenix's career was with the visionary director Paul Thomas Anderson. Their creative partnership commenced with the film "Boogie Nights" (1997), where Phoenix masterfully portrayed the troubled and emotionally vulnerable character of Jimmy. This auspicious beginning laid the foundation for a fruitful relationship that would flourish in subsequent projects.

chatvariety.com

Their collaboration reached new heights in the critically acclaimed film "The Master" (2012), which solidified their status as creative soulmates. In this profound cinematic masterpiece, Phoenix mesmerized audiences with his portrayal of the enigmatic Freddie Quell, a deeply troubled war veteran seeking solace in the charismatic teachings of a mysterious cult leader played by the late Philip Seymour Hoffman. This transformative performance by Phoenix earned him widespread acclaim, including an Academy Award nomination for Best Actor, and showcased the extraordinary synergy between Phoenix and Anderson.

Their collaboration was a creative marvel, with Anderson's masterful direction providing a canvas for Phoenix's fearless and immersive performances. Anderson's intricate and audacious storytelling intertwined seamlessly with Phoenix's ability to channel complex emotions and physicality, resulting in characters that felt fully realized and deeply human. Their partnership continued to evolve with their latest collaboration in "Inherent Vice" (2014), where Phoenix portrayed the eccentric private investigator Doc Sportello. Anderson's unique visual style and narrative intricacies weaved beautifully with Phoenix's remarkable ability to bring a character's quirks, vulnerabilities, and idiosyncrasies to life, once again leaving audiences in awe.

c h a t v a r i e t y . c o m

Another director with whom Phoenix has shared multiple collaborations is the brilliant James Gray. Their initial partnership took place in the acclaimed crime drama "The Yards" (2000), where Phoenix delivered a gritty and emotionally charged performance. This collaboration marked the beginning of a profound artistic connection that continued to bloom in subsequent projects such as "We Own the Night" (2007) and "Two Lovers" (2008). Gray's ability to craft intimate narratives with rich character development provided Phoenix with a platform to showcase his versatility as an actor.

The undeniable chemistry between Phoenix and Gray was evident in these films, as they delved into complex themes and crafted deeply human stories. Phoenix's intense and nuanced portrayals under Gray's direction drew audiences into the emotional depths of his characters. The collaboration between Phoenix and Gray is a testament to their shared commitment to exploring the complexity of the human experience and their ability to capture it on screen.

In addition to his collaborations with directors, Phoenix has had the fortune of working alongside a multitude of exceptional actors who have remarkably enhanced his performances. One of the most notable collaborations in this regard was with the late and immensely talented Philip Seymour Hoffman in "The Master". Their on-screen dynamic was a masterclass in acting, as they engaged in a gripping battle of wills, feeding off each other's energy and intensity. The profound commitment and mutual understanding between Phoenix and Hoffman forged a powerful bond that translated into captivating and deeply affecting moments throughout the film, leaving an indelible impact on audiences.

c h a t v a r i e t y . c o m

Furthermore, Phoenix's collaboration with the mesmerizing Rooney Mara in the poignant film "Her" (2013) deserves special mention. Their on-screen chemistry and profound emotional connection were essential to the success of the film, wherein Phoenix portrayed a man who develops a complex and unconventional romantic relationship with an artificial intelligence. Both Phoenix and Mara approached their roles with utmost sincerity and authenticity, infusing their performances with vulnerability, tenderness, and a genuine sense of longing. Their nuanced portrayals elevated the film to unparalleled heights and left a lasting impression on viewers.

These captivating collaborations with directors and actors have not only allowed Phoenix to showcase his remarkable range as an actor but have also pushed the boundaries of filmmaking and storytelling. His steadfast commitment to exploring diverse narratives and his willingness to collaborate with different artists have undoubtedly contributed to his reputation as a risk-taker and innovator within the industry.

As Phoenix continues to embark on new collaborations, his choices remain undeniably compelling and diverse, underscoring his unwavering dedication to challenging himself and venturing into uncharted territories. These deeply enriching partnerships have played an integral role in shaping his exceptional career and have undoubtedly solidified his status as one of the most respected and influential actors of his generation.

c h a t v a r i e t y . c o m

chatvariety.com

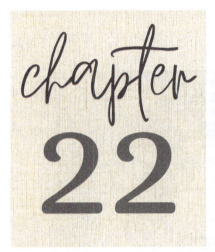
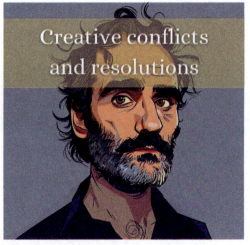

chapter 22

Creative conflicts and resolutions

Throughout his illustrious career, Joaquin Phoenix has had the opportunity to collaborate with a diverse range of directors and actors, each with their own unique vision and approach to filmmaking. While these collaborations have resulted in some of his most memorable performances, they have also brought about creative conflicts that needed to be addressed and resolved.

In the world of filmmaking, creative conflicts are not uncommon. They can stem from differences in artistic vision, disagreements on script interpretation, clashes of personalities, or even the pressures of tight production schedules. Joaquin Phoenix, known for his dedication to his craft and unyielding commitment to his characters, has found himself in several such situations, some of which have become defining moments in his career.

chatvariety.com

One notable example of a creative conflict occurred during the production of the critically acclaimed film "The Master" (2012), directed by Paul Thomas Anderson. The film delves deep into the complex relationship between a charismatic leader of a religious movement, Lancaster Dodd (played by Phoenix), and a troubled drifter, Freddie Quell (played by the late Philip Seymour Hoffman).

During the filming of "The Master," Phoenix and Anderson occasionally clashed over their interpretations of the characters and specific scenes. Phoenix, known for his immersive approach to role preparation, fully immersed himself in the psyche of Freddie Quell, portraying him as an unpredictable, volatile character. This sometimes created tension on set, as Phoenix's intense commitment clashed with Anderson's meticulous directorial style. However, both Phoenix and Anderson recognized the inherent value in their divergent perspectives and used it to push the boundaries of their creative collaboration

At the heart of creative conflicts lies the clash of artistry and the pursuit of a unified vision. In instances like these, effective communication and compromise play vital roles. Phoenix, fueled by his passion for the character and the narrative, engaged in open and honest dialogue with Anderson. They discussed their differing viewpoints, dissected the motivations of their characters, and sought to find common ground.

c h a t v a r i e t y . c o m

Anderson, known for his meticulous attention to detail and innovative storytelling, approached the project with a focus on the characters' psychological depths. Through their constructive and often intense discussions, Phoenix and Anderson navigated their creative tensions, ultimately deepening their understanding of the characters and the story they sought to tell.

This dynamic exchange of ideas allowed them to break new ground in their creative collaboration. Phoenix's immersive approach compelled Anderson to explore unexpected nuances in the characters, adding layers of complexity to their on-screen interactions. Anderson's directorial precision, on the other hand, brought out a heightened sense of structure and narrative clarity in Phoenix's performance. Their ability to harness their creative conflicts and transform them into catalysts for innovation elevated the film to new heights.

Similar conflicts and subsequent resolutions have occurred throughout Phoenix's career. They have ranged from clashes of artistic intentions on set to the challenges of collaborating with co-stars during emotionally charged scenes. In each instance, Phoenix has demonstrated his willingness to engage in open communication, actively listen to others' perspectives, and find ways to overcome creative obstacles for the betterment of the project.

These conflicts and subsequent resolutions have not only contributed to Phoenix's growth as an actor but have also elucidated the transformative power of collaboration. By confronting creative tensions head-on, Phoenix has not only expanded his range as a performer but has also developed a deeper understanding of the collaborative process and the significance of embracing differing viewpoints.

chatvariety.com

Throughout the journey of his career, Joaquin Phoenix has learned that creative conflicts are not hurdles to be avoided, but opportunities for personal and artistic growth. By embracing these conflicts and using them as catalysts for innovation, he has been able to channel his creativity into groundbreaking performances that have captivated audiences worldwide.

In the ever-evolving landscape of filmmaking, recognizing and effectively addressing creative conflicts remains crucial. By following Joaquin Phoenix's example, aspiring artists can learn the importance of honoring their creative convictions while remaining open to the perspectives and insights of their collaborators. This delicate balance allows for the harmonizing of diverse artistic visions, resulting in cinematic experiences that are not only compelling but also transformative for both creators and audiences alike.

chatvariety.com

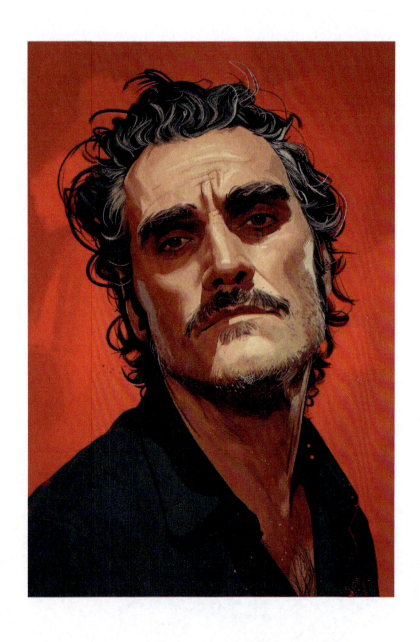

chatvariety.com

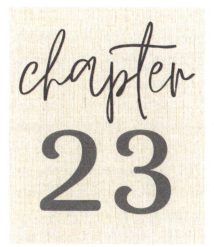 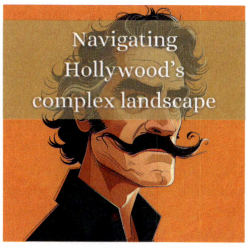

chapter 23

Navigating Hollywood's complex landscape

Navigating Hollywood's complex landscape is no easy feat, especially for an actor like Joaquin Phoenix, who has consistently challenged the status quo and prioritized artistic integrity over commercial success. Throughout his illustrious career, Phoenix has made conscious choices to work with directors and filmmakers who push the boundaries and tell unique stories. However, this approach has often led to creative conflicts, challenges in securing financing, and even controversial reactions from industry insiders.

One aspect of navigating Hollywood that Phoenix has consistently grappled with is the pressure to conform to societal norms and industry expectations. With his unconventional looks and refusal to adhere to traditional standards, Phoenix has often been met with skepticism and criticism. However, he has remained steadfast in his commitment to staying true to his artistic vision, even at the risk of being typecast or overlooked for certain roles. This unwavering dedication to authenticity has not only shaped his career but also inspired many fellow actors and artists to embrace their individuality and challenge prevailing norms.

The struggle to break free from the mold of conventional Hollywood standards has been a recurring theme in Phoenix's career. Even after achieving critical acclaim for his captivating performances, an Oscar nomination for his gripping portrayal of Johnny Cash in "Walk the Line," and finally winning the coveted award for his transformative role in "Joker," Phoenix continues to resist being pigeonholed or limited by societal expectations. His choices have reflected a commitment to exploring complex characters and unconventional narratives, often opting for roles that delve into the depths of the human psyche or shine a light on societal issues that challenge and provoke thought.

Moreover, Phoenix has had to navigate the ever-evolving dynamics of the entertainment industry. Hollywood is a constantly shifting entity, influenced by changes in audience preferences, technological advancements, and socio-cultural shifts. As an established actor, Phoenix understands the importance of staying relevant and adapting to the changing landscape. He has shown a willingness to embrace change and explore new avenues for creative expression, even as the traditional blockbuster-driven model of Hollywood gives way to the rise of streaming services and alternative platforms. While maintaining his cinematic presence, Phoenix has recently delved into the world of documentaries and executive production, associating his name with projects that amplify unheard voices and spotlight important issues.

c h a t v a r i e t y . c o m

Beyond the challenges posed by industry norms and keeping up with industry changes, Phoenix has also had to navigate the competitive nature of Hollywood. With numerous talented actors vying for limited roles, it takes more than just skill and talent to secure coveted opportunities. Networking, building relationships with influential figures, and understanding the dynamics of Hollywood are crucial in order to navigate through the competitive landscape successfully. Phoenix's ability to establish deep connections with directors, producers, and fellow actors who appreciate his dedication to his craft has not only opened doors to exciting collaborations but has also created a supportive network that nurtures his artistic growth.

To navigate the complex landscape of Hollywood, Phoenix relies on a combination of instinct, research, and collaboration. He carefully selects projects that align with his artistic sensibilities and values, going beyond the surface level of scripts to understand the deeper thematic resonance and potential for creative exploration. This meticulous approach allows him to bring his best to every role he undertakes, extracting nuance and complexity from even the most seemingly straightforward characters. His commitment to understanding the nuances of his characters goes beyond the script, often immersing himself in extensive research to truly embody the essence of each role.

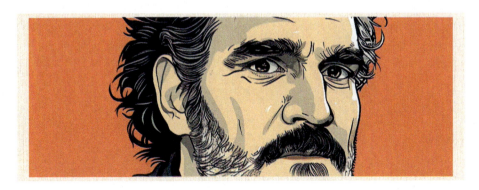

c h a t v a r i e t y . c o m

Phoenix's journey in Hollywood is also intertwined with the politics and power dynamics of the industry. Hollywood is notorious for its hierarchies, gatekeepers, and favoritism. In order to gain recognition and secure desirable roles, actors must navigate these nuances carefully, often relying on personal connections and strategic decision-making. However, Phoenix has never been one to actively chase awards or accolades, instead focusing on the art itself. This approach has given him a sense of freedom and independence, allowing him to make creative choices without the burden of external validation. By remaining true to his vision and embracing his artistic calling, Phoenix has proven that success can be achieved on his own terms.

Furthermore, Hollywood is an industry that thrives on trends and marketability. It is often driven by financial considerations rather than artistic merit. Phoenix, with his inclination towards unconventional and challenging projects, has found it necessary to balance his artistic integrity with the realities of the industry. This delicate balance requires careful decision-making, strategic choices, and an understanding of audience expectations. While he continues to seek out projects that fulfill him artistically, he also recognizes the need to stay mindful of the commercial viability of his endeavors, allowing him to reach larger audiences and amplify his artistic message.

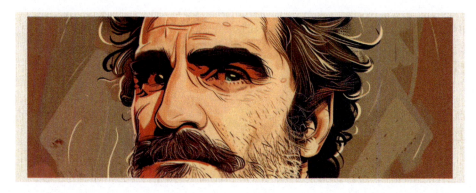

c h a t v a r i e t y . c o m

In conclusion, navigating Hollywood's complex landscape has been an intricate journey for Joaquin Phoenix throughout his career. From facing skepticism and criticism for his unconventional approach to grappling with industry politics, power dynamics, and the ever-evolving nature of the entertainment industry, Phoenix has managed to navigate these challenges with grace and authenticity. By staying true to his artistic vision, building meaningful relationships with like-minded collaborators, and carefully selecting projects that strike a balance between artistic fulfillment and commercial viability, Phoenix has carved out a unique space for himself in the industry. His ability to navigate through the complexities and tensions of Hollywood is a testament to his resilience, unwavering commitment to his craft, and his passion for pushing artistic boundaries. It serves as an inspiration to fellow artists who strive to navigate the intricate web of the entertainment industry while maintaining their artistic integrity.

chatvariety.com

chatvariety.com

CHAPTER 8: LEGACY AND INFLUENCE

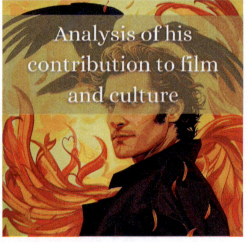

chapter 24

Analysis of his contribution to film and culture

Joaquin Phoenix has undeniably left an indelible mark on the world of film and culture through his exceptional talent and compelling performances. His contribution to both the art form and the societal impact of cinema cannot be understated. In this chapter, we will delve into the various aspects of his work and explore the profound influence he has had on the industry.

From the beginning of his career, Phoenix exhibited a profound commitment to his craft and a willingness to take on challenging and unconventional roles. This dedication allowed him to transcend the boundaries of traditional acting and become a transformative force on screen. His choices of projects, often leaning towards thought-provoking and socially relevant narratives, have further exemplified his commitment to using his platform to contribute to meaningful storytelling.

chatvariety.com

One of the key elements of Phoenix's contribution to film lies in his ability to fully immerse himself in his characters. Known for his intense method acting techniques, he delves deep into the psyche of the individuals he portrays. This dedication to authenticity resonates with audiences, providing them with a glimpse into the emotional depths of the human experience. Through his meticulous research, he strives to understand the background, motivations, and intricacies of each character, allowing him to convincingly bring them to life on screen. Such dedication to his craft speaks not only to his exceptional acting skills but also to his unwavering commitment to telling stories that resonate with audiences on a profound level.

Phoenix's artistry extends beyond the realm of acting. He has also ventured into other areas of the filmmaking process, including producing and directing. These ventures showcase his multifaceted talent and his desire to explore new creative avenues. As a producer, he actively seeks out stories that challenge norms and bring marginalized narratives to the forefront. Through his production company, he has supported projects such as "The Sisters Brothers" and "Don't Worry, He Won't Get Far on Foot," which spotlight the unconventional and explore themes of redemption and resilience. As a director, his efforts, including the influential documentary "Earthlings," demonstrate his commitment to using his creativity to shed light on important social issues while advocating for empathy, compassion, and sustainable living.

c h a t v a r i e t y . c o m

Furthermore, the impact of Phoenix's performances goes beyond the silver screen. His roles often tackle important societal issues, shining a light on topics such as mental health, addiction, and social injustice. By fearlessly embodying characters dealing with these challenges, Phoenix not only humanizes their struggles but also raises awareness and fosters conversations around these critical subjects. His portrayal of Arthur Fleck in "Joker," for example, not only showcased his exceptional acting abilities but also sparked discussions about the marginalization of mental health issues and the consequences of societal neglect. Through his portrayals, he encourages empathy, understanding, and the urgent need for change.

In addition to his artistic contributions, Phoenix's philanthropic endeavors have made a significant impact on the world. His dedication to animal rights and environmental issues has led him to actively support various organizations and initiatives. By leveraging his fame and influence, he has inspired others to take action and make a difference. From his heartfelt acceptance speeches at award ceremonies to his decision to wear sustainable fashion on the red carpet, Phoenix consistently uses his platform to highlight the urgency of environmental conservation and the ethical treatment of animals. In doing so, he has become a powerful advocate for positive change, inspiring others to examine their own choices and contribute towards a more sustainable and compassionate world.

Analyzing Phoenix's contribution to film and culture also requires acknowledging his enduring legacy. His body of work will continue to resonate with audiences for generations to come. His ability to inhabit complex characters and challenge societal norms has paved the way for future actors and filmmakers to push creative boundaries and tell compelling stories. Phoenix's influence can already be seen in the increased recognition of independent and character-driven films, as well as the incorporation of social commentary in mainstream cinema. As aspiring artists and moviegoers alike study his performances and insights, they will undoubtedly be inspired to contribute their unique voices to further the evolution of film and culture.

In conclusion, Joaquin Phoenix's contribution to film and culture is multi-faceted and far-reaching. Through his exceptional talent, immersive performances, and commitment to social issues, he has left an indelible mark in the industry. Phoenix's legacy will continue to shape the landscape of cinema, inspiring future generations to fearlessly explore the depths of storytelling, challenge societal norms, and make a positive impact on the world through the power of film.

chatvariety.com

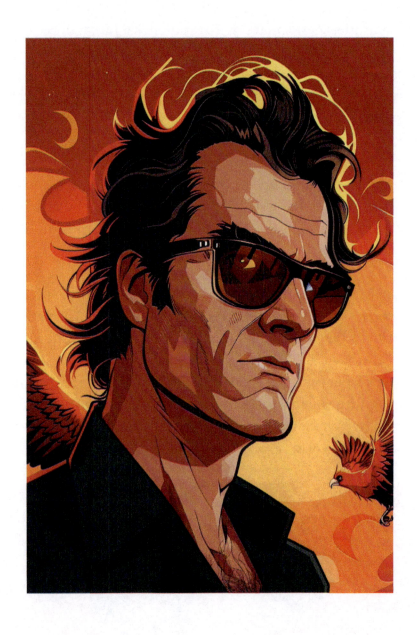

chatvariety.com

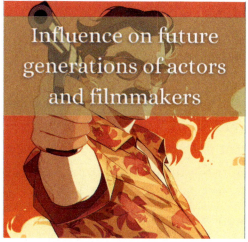

chapter 25

Influence on future generations of actors and filmmakers

Joaquin Phoenix's impact on the world of acting and filmmaking goes beyond his own performances and achievements, permeating the very essence of the craft and inspiring future generations of artists. His dedication to his craft, his fearless approach to challenging roles, and his ability to truly inhabit the characters he portrays have set a new standard for aspiring actors, elevating the art form itself.

One of the most profound ways in which Phoenix has influenced future actors is through his unwavering commitment to method acting. This approach, which involves fully immersing oneself in a character's emotions, physicality, and psyche, allows actors to create deeply layered and authentic performances. Phoenix has masterfully demonstrated the transformative power of method acting throughout his career. From his haunting portrayal of Arthur Fleck in "Joker," to his mesmerizing embodiment of Johnny Cash in "Walk the Line," Phoenix has consistently pushed the boundaries of what can be achieved through this technique. His dedication and meticulous attention to the smallest details inspire young actors to delve into the depths of their characters, to explore the complexities of human emotions, and to find greater authenticity in their own portrayals.

Moreover, Phoenix's ability to bring a sense of unwavering authenticity and vulnerability to his performances has resonated deeply with audiences and fellow artists alike. There is a rawness and honesty to his work that is truly captivating. Whether he is exploring the struggles of mental health, the complexities of love and relationships, or the inner demons that haunt individuals, Phoenix has an unparalleled ability to tap into the universal human experience. Through his genuine and nuanced portrayals, he has created characters that feel undeniably real, forging deep connections with audiences on a profound level. His willingness to expose his own vulnerabilities on screen has not only pushed the boundaries of his own craft but has also opened the door for other actors to embrace their own imperfections, encouraging a new generation of performers to explore the more complex and nuanced aspects of human nature.

Furthermore, Phoenix's collaborations with visionary filmmakers have had a significant impact on the future of the craft. Working with directors such as Paul Thomas Anderson and Spike Jonze, he has not only delivered exceptional performances but has also challenged the traditional norms of storytelling and filmmaking. Phoenix's ability to seamlessly transition across different genres and styles brings a unique and captivating energy to each project, consistently leaving an indelible mark on the art form. Directors have been inspired by his commitment to the craft, his willingness to experiment with different techniques, and his ability to breathe life into even the most unconventional characters. Through his collaborations, he has helped redefine the boundaries of storytelling, inspiring future filmmakers to think outside the box and explore new realms of creativity.

c h a t v a r i e t y . c o m

Beyond his impact on the craft itself, Phoenix has also made a significant contribution through his activism. His advocacy for animal rights, environmental causes, and social justice has inspired a new generation of artists to use their platform for positive change. Through his passion and dedication, Phoenix has shown that artists can make a difference and use their influence to raise awareness and promote important causes. His acceptance speeches at prestigious award ceremonies have become rallying cries for social change, shedding light on pressing issues and calling for collective action. By using his fame to amplify the voices of the marginalized and underrepresented, Phoenix has ignited a fire within aspiring actors and filmmakers to actively engage in social justice, recognizing the transformative power of art.

In concluding, Joaquin Phoenix's influence on future generations of actors and filmmakers is immeasurable. By continually pushing the boundaries of his craft, he has redefined what it means to be an actor, reminding us that acting is not simply an exercise in pretense, but a profound exploration of the human condition. His commitment to embodying the truth of each character has allowed him to delve into the depths of humanity, illuminating the emotions, struggles, and triumphs that connect us all. As aspiring actors and filmmakers look to Phoenix as a beacon of creativity, authenticity, and social consciousness, they will undoubtedly continue to shape the industry, further redefining the boundaries of what can be achieved in cinema and leaving a lasting legacy for future generations to come.

c h a t v a r i e t y . c o m

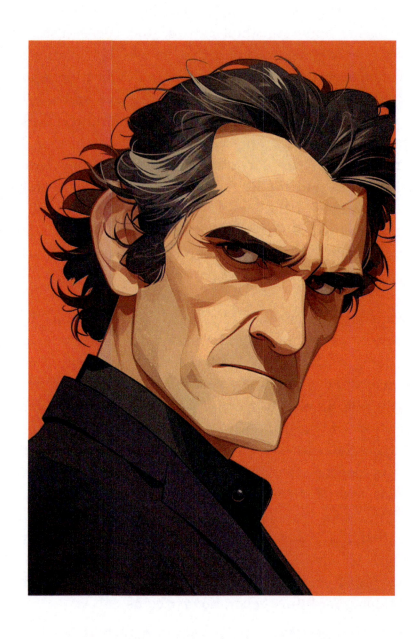

chatvariety.com

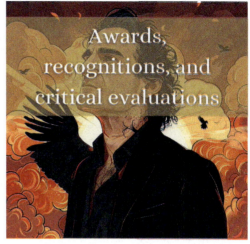

chapter 26

Awards, recognitions, and critical evaluations

Joaquin Phoenix's remarkable career has been celebrated with numerous awards, recognitions, and critical evaluations from both the industry and the public. His journey from child actor to Hollywood A-lister has been marked by exceptional performances that have garnered widespread acclaim and prestigious accolades.

One of the earliest recognitions of Phoenix's talent came in 2000 when he received an Academy Award nomination for Best Supporting Actor for his role as Commodus in Ridley Scott's epic film "Gladiator." Although he did not win the award, this nomination marked the beginning of a pattern of recognition that would follow him throughout his career.

In 2006, Phoenix once again received an Academy Award nomination, this time for his transformative portrayal of Johnny Cash in "Walk the Line." Directed by James Mangold, the film chronicled the life of the legendary musician, and Phoenix's dedication to his craft shone through as he captivated audiences with his raw and authentic depiction of Cash. This performance garnered critical acclaim and further solidified his place as a leading actor in the industry.

c h a t v a r i e t y . c o m

It was in 2020 that Phoenix's talent was finally honored with the most prestigious award in the film industry – the Academy Award for Best Actor. His captivating and haunting portrayal of Arthur Fleck, a mentally troubled man who becomes the iconic Joker, left a profound impact on audiences worldwide. Directed by Todd Phillips, "Joker" explored the darker aspects of society and the human psyche, and Phoenix's performance resonated deeply with viewers. The award not only recognized his exceptional acting skills but also acknowledged his enduring contributions to cinema.

While the Academy Awards hold immense significance, they are not the only measure of Phoenix's talent and impact. Throughout his career, he has received numerous other accolades, including Golden Globe Awards, BAFTA Awards, Screen Actors Guild Awards, and many more. These awards reflect the industry's recognition of his outstanding performances and his ability to breathe life into diverse characters.

In addition to the formal recognition he has received, Phoenix's work has garnered critical acclaim and respect from film critics. They praise his ability to wholly immerse himself in each role, showing a remarkable range and a profound understanding of his characters. He fearlessly embraces complex and challenging roles, whether it's as the troubled Theodore in Spike Jonze's thought-provoking film "Her," the tortured Freddie Quell in Paul Thomas Anderson's "The Master," or the relentless mercenary Joe in Lynne Ramsay's intense thriller "You Were Never Really Here." These performances have demonstrated Phoenix's versatility and willingness to tackle unconventional narratives and explore the depths of the human condition.

chatvariety.com

Furthermore, Phoenix's work extends beyond entertainment; it has the power to spark essential dialogues and shed light on pressing societal issues. In films such as "We Own the Night," he explores the devastating impact of drug addiction, delving into the complexities of the human struggle. In "Two Lovers," Phoenix immerses himself in the portrayal of a man battling mental health challenges, offering a sensitive portrayal that destigmatizes these often misunderstood conditions. His performances have brought attention to these issues, fostering empathy and understanding among audiences.

Phoenix's portrayal of Arthur Fleck in "Joker" also ignited conversations surrounding mental health, the marginalization of certain individuals, and the consequences of a society that fails to support its vulnerable members. His commitment to depicting the complexities of mental illness with nuance and authenticity resonated with viewers who were moved by his portrayal. Through this film, Phoenix highlighted the importance of addressing mental health issues with compassion and empathy.

In addition to raising awareness through his performances, Phoenix has utilized his platform for political activism and to advocate for social change. His acceptance speeches, including a powerful speech at the 2020 Academy Awards, delivered impassioned messages about animal rights, environmental conservation, and systemic inequalities. Phoenix's willingness to use his fame as a force for good has further solidified his standing as an influential and socially conscious artist.

chatvariety.com

His dedication and activism extend to his personal life as well. Phoenix has been a longtime vegan and has actively campaigned against the mistreatment of animals. His passionate stance on animal rights led to his collaboration with animal advocacy organizations, and he has used his fame to draw attention to the importance of compassionate living.

Phoenix's influence as an artist has also inspired collaborations with visionary directors who recognize his unparalleled talent. Filmmakers are drawn to his ability to transform into complex characters, allowing the audience to deeply connect with the stories being told. This collaboration is evident in his work with renowned directors such as Paul Thomas Anderson, Spike Jonze, and Todd Phillips, among others.

In conclusion, Joaquin Phoenix's career has been filled with awards, recognitions, and critical evaluations that collectively highlight his exceptional talent and contributions to the film industry. His transformative performances, commitment to his craft, and willingness to tackle complex characters have earned him the highest honors and the respect of his peers. Beyond awards, his work continues to inspire and resonate with audiences worldwide, instigating important conversations about societal issues and shining a light on the human experience. Phoenix's legacy as one of the most accomplished and influential actors of our time is solidified through his tireless dedication to his craft, his passion for making a positive impact on the world, and his collaborations with visionary directors who recognize his exceptional talent.

c h a t v a r i e t y . c o m

CHAPTER 9: THE PHOENIX PHENOMENON

chapter 27

The symbolism of rebirth in his career

Joaquin Phoenix's career has been marked by a series of transformative moments, both on and off-screen. One powerful symbolism that runs through his journey is the concept of rebirth. Like a phoenix rising from the ashes, Phoenix has experienced numerous personal and professional setbacks, only to emerge stronger and more committed to his craft.

Throughout his career, Phoenix has demonstrated an ability to reinvent himself, shedding old identities and embracing new challenges. This continuous process of transformation mirrors the cycle of rebirth, where the old is left behind to make way for the new. It is this willingness to let go of familiar territories and dive into uncharted waters that sets Phoenix apart as an actor.

Notably, the symbolism of rebirth is also evident in the roles Phoenix has chosen to portray on-screen. His characters often undergo profound personal transformations, navigating emotional turmoil, and transcending their limitations. These journeys mirror Phoenix's own path of self-discovery and growth, allowing him to connect with audiences on a deep and resonant level.

chatvariety.com

Consider his role as Arthur Fleck in "Joker," a film that explores the descent into madness and the reemergence as a formidable force. In this role, Phoenix's transformation is not just physical, but also psychological. He delves into the depths of Arthur's tortured psyche, revealing a man on the brink of self-destruction. Through his portrayal, Phoenix embodies the concept of rebirth as Arthur rises from the ashes of his former self to become an agent of chaos and transformation.

Moreover, the concept of rebirth is intricately tied to the notion of redemption, a theme that frequently appears in Phoenix's films. His characters often grapple with inner demons, seeking salvation and a chance at redemption. Through their struggles, Phoenix explores the human capacity for change and the possibility of finding redemption in even the most unlikely circumstances.

In "The Master," Phoenix portrays Freddie Quell, a troubled and volatile navy veteran who finds himself entangled in the web of a charismatic cult leader. As Freddie embarks on a quest for belonging and purpose, he undergoes a profound transformation, navigating the complexities of power dynamics and his own internal conflicts. Through Phoenix's nuanced performance, we witness the rebirth of Freddie's spirit, as he confronts his past and finds a glimmer of hope for redemption.

Off-screen, Phoenix's personal journey reflects a similar process of rebirth. He has been very open about his battles with addiction and personal demons, acknowledging his own flaws and embracing the opportunity for self-improvement. This vulnerability and authenticity have endeared him to fans and critics alike, further solidifying his status as a transformative figure in the industry.

c h a t v a r i e t y . c o m

Indeed, Phoenix's commitment to social and environmental causes also mirrors his symbolic rebirth. In recent years, he has used his platform to advocate for animal rights and environmental conservation. Through his passionate activism, Phoenix showcases the transformative power of empathy and compassion, calling for a collective rebirth in our relationship with the natural world.

The symbolism of rebirth in Phoenix's career serves as a reminder that setbacks and challenges are not the end but rather an opportunity for growth and reinvention. It is through these moments of rebirth that Phoenix has continuously evolved as an actor and as an individual, pushing the boundaries of his craft and inspiring others to do the same.

Rebirth, however, is not a linear journey. It is a constant process of self-reflection, self-discovery, and adaptation. Phoenix's evolution is evident in his willingness to step outside his comfort zone and take on roles that challenge societal norms and conventions. From his raw and intimate portrayal of Johnny Cash in "Walk the Line" to his captivating depiction of a volatile hitman in "You Were Never Really Here," Phoenix consistently pushes himself to explore the depths of human emotions and experiences.

The symbolic rebirth in Phoenix's career can also be seen in his collaborations with visionary directors. From working with Paul Thomas Anderson in "The Master" to teaming up with Todd Phillips in "Joker," Phoenix enters into creative partnerships that challenge his skills and stretch his artistic boundaries. These collaborations act as catalysts for his growth, allowing him to dig deeper into his characters and bring forth nuanced performances that leave a lasting impact.

In addition to his acting prowess, Phoenix's commitment to authenticity further enhances the symbolism of rebirth in his career. He immerses himself fully into his roles, often undergoing physical and emotional transformations to embody his characters. Whether it is losing weight, learning new skills, or delving into intense research, Phoenix dedicates himself to the craft with unwavering devotion, symbolizing a constant rebirth of dedication and discipline.

As we witness the ongoing journey of Joaquin Phoenix, it becomes evident that the symbolism of rebirth will continue to shape his career. It acts as a guiding force, propelling him to new heights and encouraging him to explore uncharted territories. Just as a phoenix rises from the ashes, Phoenix embraces the power of transformation and uses it to ignite the screen with his exceptional performances.

In conclusion, the symbolism of rebirth in Joaquin Phoenix's career is a testament to his resilience, dedication, and commitment to the craft of acting. It serves as a powerful reminder that true growth and transformation can arise from even the darkest moments. As we eagerly anticipate what the future holds for this remarkable actor, we can be sure that his journey of rebirth will continue to captivate and inspire audiences around the world.

c h a t v a r i e t y . c o m

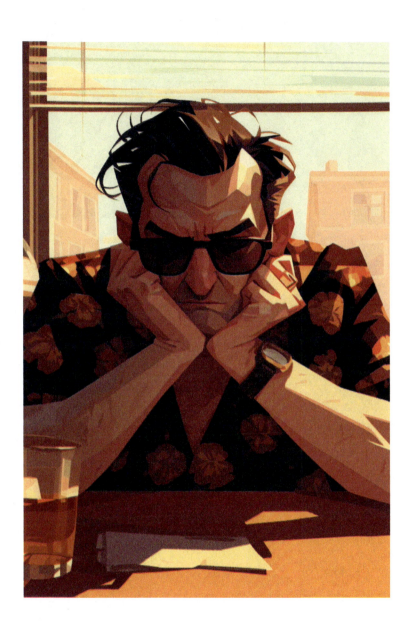

chatvariety.com

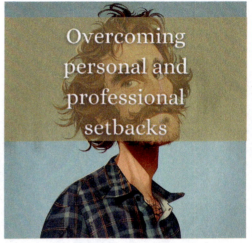

chapter 28
Overcoming personal and professional setbacks

Joaquin Phoenix's journey as an actor and individual has not been without its fair share of setbacks. Like many artists, he has faced personal and professional challenges throughout his career. However, it is his ability to overcome these obstacles that truly sets him apart.

On a personal level, Joaquin Phoenix has struggled with mental health issues and addiction. In the past, he was open about his battle with alcoholism and his subsequent journey to sobriety. These struggles not only took a toll on his personal life but also affected his professional opportunities. There were times when his behavior was erratic, leading to strained relationships with directors, producers, and fellow actors.

Phoenix's battle with addiction is a deeply rooted part of his story. It is a reminder that even those in the spotlight, with fame and success at their fingertips, can still struggle with internal demons. Addiction is a disease that does not discriminate, and Phoenix's openness about his struggle serves as a beacon of hope and inspiration for others who may share similar struggles.

chatvariety.com

In addition to his personal challenges, Phoenix faced professional setbacks as well. After his early success in films like "To Die For" and "Gladiator," he found himself trapped in the confines of being typecast as intense and brooding characters. This pigeonholing limited his choices and prevented him from exploring a wider range of roles that showcased his true versatility as an actor.

The art of acting lies in the ability to transform oneself, to become someone else entirely. For Joaquin Phoenix, breaking free from the limitations of typecasting became a vital part of his artistic evolution. It took bravery and determination to step away from the roles that brought him initial success and instead pursue projects that would challenge him on a deeper level. This decision to break free from the mold allowed Phoenix to redefine himself as an actor and unlock a new dimension of his talent.

However, it was his decision to take a break from acting and venture into music with the experimental mockumentary "I'm Still Here" that truly marked a turning point in Phoenix's career. The film, directed by Casey Affleck, deeply blurred the lines between reality and fiction. It followed Phoenix's supposed spiral into a world of eccentricity and self-destructive behavior.

The film received mixed reviews, with many questioning whether Phoenix had truly gone off the deep end or if it was all an elaborate performance art piece. Regardless of the audience's interpretation, "I'm Still Here" served as a catalyst for Phoenix's personal and professional growth. It allowed him to shed the constraints of his previous image and embark on a journey of self-discovery and reinvention.

chatvariety.com

During his hiatus from acting, Phoenix underwent a profound transformation, both physically and emotionally. He gained weight and grew a disheveled beard, completely immersing himself in the character he was trying to create. This commitment to his craft showcased his unparalleled dedication and willingness to push the boundaries of his comfort zone.

When Phoenix returned to acting, he did so with a renewed focus and a fresh perspective. His astonishing performance as Freddie Quell in "The Master" not only solidified his place as one of the most talented actors of his generation but also earned him critical acclaim and numerous awards. With every project he took on, Phoenix demonstrated his range and versatility, successfully shedding the labels that had once confined him.

Perhaps the pinnacle of Phoenix's career came with his portrayal of Arthur Fleck in "Joker." This role was a true tour de force, pushing the boundaries of his own sanity and immersing himself in the depths of a broken mind. Phoenix's commitment to understanding and humanizing this complex character resulted in a performance that shook audiences to their core. It was a portrayal that transcended the superhero genre and cemented Phoenix's legacy as one of the greatest actors of his time.

Phoenix's ability to overcome personal and professional setbacks can be attributed to his resilience and willingness to challenge himself. He learned from his past mistakes and used them as catalysts for growth. Rather than letting setbacks define him, he embraced them as opportunities for reinvention.

By triumphing over adversity, Joaquin Phoenix has become an inspiration to many. His story serves as a reminder that setbacks are not permanent roadblocks but merely temporary detours on the path to success. Through his resilience and determination, he has proven that personal and professional setbacks can be overcome, and they can even become stepping stones towards a brighter future.

Joaquin Phoenix's journey of overcoming setbacks is a testament to his unwavering passion for his craft. It is a testimony to his ability to learn and grow from difficult experiences, ultimately emerging stronger and more resilient. His story serves as a reminder that success is not always a linear progression, but rather a series of trials and triumphs that shape an artist's legacy. And in Phoenix's case, these setbacks have only fueled his artistic fire, propelling him to even greater heights and solidifying his place among the pantheon of great actors.

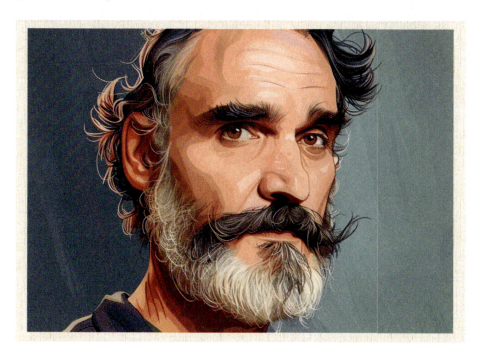

chatvariety.com

chatvariety.com

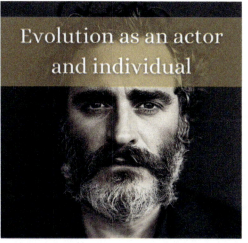

chapter 29

Evolution as an actor and individual

Joaquin Phoenix's evolution as an actor and individual has been an extraordinary journey of self-discovery, artistic exploration, and profound personal growth. Throughout his illustrious career, Phoenix has continuously pushed the boundaries of his craft and embraced diverse roles that challenge both his artistic capabilities and his own understanding of the human experience. However, it is not just his acting abilities that have undergone a transformation; Phoenix's personal journey and the values he espouses have played a significant role in shaping him into the remarkable artist and advocate he is today.

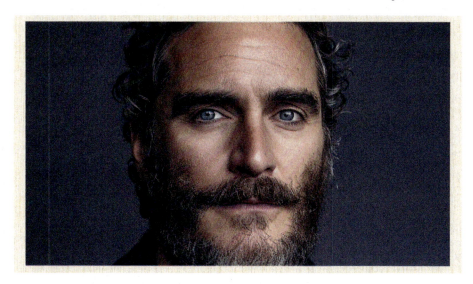

chatvariety.com

One of the most remarkable aspects of Phoenix's evolution is his unwavering commitment to taking risks and embracing unconventional roles. From his early breakthrough as a child actor to his groundbreaking performances in films such as "The Master" and "Joker," Phoenix has consistently demonstrated a willingness to delve deep into the complexities of characters and narratives that challenge societal norms. He seeks out projects that are intellectually stimulating, emotionally demanding, and provide ample room for artistic exploration. By choosing to portray characters as diverse as Johnny Cash, Commodus, and Arthur Fleck, Phoenix has time and again showcased his immense versatility and range, proving that he can breathe life into any character with unparalleled precision and authenticity.

Central to Phoenix's evolution as an actor and individual is his intense dedication to research and preparation for each role. He fully immerses himself in the lives of his characters, spending extensive time understanding their motivations, behavioral patterns, and inner struggles. This meticulous approach enables Phoenix to bring an unparalleled level of depth to his performances. Whether it is adopting the idiosyncrasies of John Callahan in "Don't Worry, He Won't Get Far on Foot" or transforming his physique and internalizing the torment of Arthur Fleck in "Joker," Phoenix's unwavering commitment to authenticity has earned him immense critical acclaim and numerous prestigious awards.

c h a t v a r i e t y . c o m

Nonetheless, Phoenix's evolution goes beyond his professional life; it is intricately intertwined with his personal growth. The turning point in his personal journey came with his decision to embrace a vegan lifestyle, one driven by his ardent advocacy for animal rights, environmental sustainability, and social justice. Phoenix's beliefs inform not only his personal choices but also his platform as a globally recognized figure, using his influence to raise awareness and incite positive change. His speeches on inclusivity, compassion, and the urgency to address urgent global issues have resonated with audiences worldwide, further establishing him as a true artist with a social conscience.

Moreover, his choice to adopt a vegan lifestyle not only reflects his commitment to ethical living but also speaks to his profound connection with nature and the environment. Phoenix recognizes that the choices we make as individuals have ripple effects that impact not just our own lives but the entire planet. Through his advocacy for sustainable practices and conservation efforts, he highlights the importance of living in harmony with the natural world, to protect and preserve it for future generations.

Furthermore, Phoenix's evolution as an actor and individual is intrinsically linked to his commitment to confront and overcome personal challenges. Throughout his life, he has been candid about his struggles with addiction and mental health. These battles have tested his resilience and fortitude, but instead of letting them define him, Phoenix has channeled these experiences into a catalyst for growth and self-reflection. Through therapy, sobriety, and constant introspection, he has gained valuable insights into the complexities of the human condition, fueling his performances with a raw vulnerability and emotional depth that resonates with audiences on a profound level.

Phoenix's journey as an actor and individual is not confined to the silver screen or his personal life; it extends to his vision for a more inclusive and equitable society. He uses his platform to champion the causes close to his heart, advocating for marginalized communities, speaking out against social injustices, and encouraging empathy and understanding among people. In doing so, he amplifies voices that are often silenced and inspires others to join him in forging a more compassionate world.

What sets Phoenix apart from other actors is not just his willingness to evolve but his ability to surprise and captivate viewers with each new project. Whether he is channeling the raw intensity of Commodus in "Gladiator" or embodying the poetic frailty of Freddie Quell in "The Master," Phoenix is a constant revelation, continually challenging himself and pushing the envelope of his boundless talent. His evolution as an actor and individual is not limited to a linear trajectory; rather, it is an ongoing, lifelong journey of self-discovery and artistic exploration.

c h a t v a r i e t y . c o m

In conclusion, Joaquin Phoenix's evolution as an actor and individual is a testament to his unwavering commitment to growth, both personally and professionally. From his early beginnings as a child actor to his transformative performances in recent years, Phoenix has embraced the complexities inherent in every character, presenting humanity's multifaceted nature onscreen. Through his personal journey and dedication to promoting meaningful change, he has become an influential figure whose impact transcends the realm of entertainment. As Joaquin Phoenix continues to evolve as an actor and individual, audiences can anticipate being captivated, challenged, and moved by his performances for years to come.

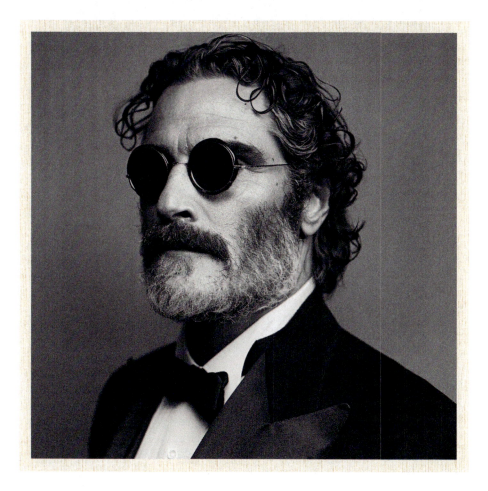

c h a t v a r i e t y . c o m

chatvariety.com

CHAPTER 10: A PHOENIX RISEN

chatvariety.com

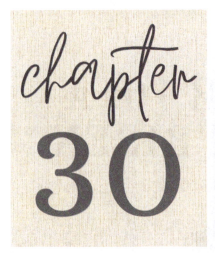
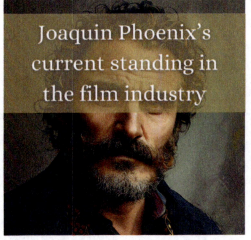

chapter 30

Joaquin Phoenix's current standing in the film industry

Joaquin Phoenix's current standing in the film industry can only be described as remarkable. After decades of hard work, dedication, and a series of unforgettable performances, Phoenix has solidified his position as one of the most talented and respected actors of his generation.

Born on October 28, 1974, in San Juan, Puerto Rico, Joaquin Phoenix's journey to stardom has been marked by both triumph and tragedy. Coming from a family of performers, he and his siblings were raised in a nomadic environment, traveling across South America as part of the religious group known as the Children of God. This unconventional upbringing had a profound impact on Phoenix, shaping his worldview and fueling his desire to explore the depths of human emotions through his acting.

Phoenix's career began in the early 1980s, appearing in television shows and made-for-TV movies. His talent and dedication soon caught the attention of industry professionals, leading to his breakout role in Ron Howard's film "Parenthood" (1989). Despite being just 14 years old at the time, Phoenix delivered a nuanced performance that showcased his ability to portray complex emotions with maturity beyond his years.

chatvariety.com

However, tragedy struck in 1993 when Phoenix's older brother, River Phoenix, passed away at the age of 23 due to a drug overdose. The loss had a profound impact on Joaquin and his family, leaving an indelible mark on his artistic journey. It was during this difficult period that Joaquin took a hiatus from acting, seeking solace and time to heal.

When he returned to the screen, Phoenix's performances began to delve deeper into the human psyche, revealing a profound understanding of complex characters. His collaboration with director M. Night Shyamalan in "Signs" (2002) demonstrated his ability to effortlessly encapsulate a character's inner turmoil while providing moments of vulnerability and introspection. This role further contributed to his growing reputation as an actor capable of bringing depth and authenticity to his characters.

Phoenix solidified his status as a versatile actor with his remarkable portrayal of Johnny Cash in "Walk the Line" (2005). Immersing himself fully into the role, Phoenix transformed into the iconic musician, mastering Cash's distinctive vocal style and capturing the essence of his turbulent life. Through his powerful performance, he not only earned critical acclaim and numerous accolades but also earned the respect of his peers and industry veterans.

chatvariety.com

Continuing to push the boundaries of his craft, Phoenix's collaboration with director Paul Thomas Anderson in "The Master" (2012) showcased his ability to embody complex and psychologically tortured characters. As Freddie Quell, a tormented World War II veteran drawn into a religious cult, Phoenix delivered a riveting performance that left audiences mesmerized. His immersion into the character was so profound that it became difficult to distinguish Phoenix from the troubled Freddie Quell, earning him his third Academy Award nomination.

In recent years, Phoenix's collaboration with director Todd Phillips on "Joker" (2019) brought his immense talent to an even wider audience. Playing the titular character, Phoenix fully immersed himself in the mind of Arthur Fleck, portraying the descent into madness of a lonely and alienated man. His ability to create a sense of empathy for the character while exploring the darker aspects of the human condition was hailed as a masterclass in acting. The role ultimately earned Phoenix his first Academy Award for Best Actor and elevated him to an even higher echelon of revered actors.

Beyond his on-screen accomplishments, Phoenix's dedication to using his platform for positive change has become an integral part of his persona. He is an advocate for animal rights and has been instrumental in raising awareness about the cruelty associated with the farming of animals for fashion. In addition, his commitment to environmental conservation has led him to lead a vegan lifestyle and speak out against deforestation and climate change. Phoenix's speeches and actions have resonated with fans and non-fans alike, further solidifying his reputation as an artist with a social conscience.

Looking forward, Joaquin Phoenix's current standing promises an exciting future. His dedication to his craft, willingness to take risks, and ability to seamlessly merge into complex characters have ignited anticipation for his upcoming projects. Audiences and industry professionals alike eagerly await the next transformation that Phoenix will undertake, as they know he is not one to rest on his laurels.

In conclusion, Joaquin Phoenix's current standing in the film industry remains that of a revered and influential actor. Through his remarkable performances, personal growth, and commitment to creating positive change, Phoenix has left an indelible mark on the industry. Joaquin Phoenix's talent, resilience, and advocacy ensure that his standing will endure, serving as an inspiration for aspiring actors and a benchmark for excellence in acting.

chatvariety.com

chatvariety.com

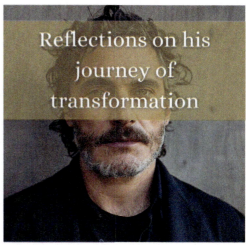

Reflections on his journey of transformation

Throughout his illustrious career, Joaquin Phoenix has undergone tremendous personal and professional growth, leading to a profound transformation both as an actor and as an individual. As he reflects on his journey, he finds himself in awe of the path he has taken and the challenges he has overcome.

One of the key elements of Phoenix's transformation has been his unwavering dedication to his craft. From an early age, he displayed an extraordinary commitment to fully embodying the characters he portrays on screen. It is this deep immersion into each role that requires an immense amount of vulnerability and self-exploration, pushing Phoenix to confront his own inner demons and fears.

In his reflections, Phoenix acknowledges the role that his early struggles and rejections played in shaping his determination. The disappointments and missed opportunities forced him to reevaluate his approach to acting, leading him to commit even more passionately to his art. Through these experiences, he discovered the importance of continuous growth and never settling for mediocrity.

Beneath the surface of every character he brings to life lies a complex tapestry of emotions and experiences. Phoenix understands that to create truly impactful performances, he must delve deep into the psyche of his characters, unearthing their complexities and finding the raw truths that lie beneath. This process demands not only an understanding of the character's motivations but also a journey into his own emotions and vulnerabilities.

In his quest for authenticity, Phoenix has embraced the highs and lows of his own journey. He has grappled with his own personal demons, battling addiction and navigating the complexities of mental health. These struggles have been well-documented, but Phoenix views them not as setbacks but as opportunities for growth. It is through these very challenges that he has found a deeper understanding of himself and his craft. He believes that these experiences have given him a unique perspective on life and have enriched his ability to empathize with the characters he portrays.

The transformative power of his roles cannot be overstated. Phoenix's dedication to pushing boundaries has reshaped the landscape of cinema. From his portrayal of the tormented Arthur Fleck in "Joker" to his mesmerizing performance as Johnny Cash in "Walk the Line," each character has allowed Phoenix to explore facets of his own identity, unlocking hidden emotions and capabilities that he never knew existed.

c h a t v a r i e t y . c o m

But it is not only within the realm of acting that Phoenix has experienced transformation. He has also evolved as an individual, learning to navigate the pressures of fame and the ever-changing landscape of Hollywood. Through it all, he has remained grounded and true to his values, using his platform to shed light on important social and environmental issues. Phoenix understands the influence he wields and recognizes the responsibility that comes with it. His passion for animal rights and his strong advocacy for environmental causes have earned him respect and admiration far beyond the silver screen.

As he looks back on his remarkable transformation, Phoenix is filled with gratitude for the opportunities he has been given and the support he has received along the way. The love and appreciation from his fans have fueled his drive to continually reinvent himself and push the boundaries of his art. This constant evolution and introspection have brought him to new heights of artistic achievement, and he cherishes every moment of his journey, the triumphs and setbacks alike.

His journey of transformation has also brought about a deeper sense of purpose. Phoenix understands that his influence extends far beyond the realm of entertainment, and he is committed to using his voice and platform for meaningful change. He actively engages with organizations and advocates for social justice, equality, and sustainability. His belief in the power of storytelling as a means of creating empathy and understanding shines through his work and his philanthropic efforts.

chatvariety.com

As he continues to evolve, Phoenix is excited about the future challenges and triumphs that lie ahead. He recognizes that the journey of transformation is never complete, as there is always more to learn, explore, and discover. He is open to new opportunities that push him out of his comfort zone and compel him to grow as an artist and a human being.

In conclusion, Joaquin Phoenix's journey of transformation is a testament to the power of perseverance, self-reflection, and dedication to one's craft. Through his immersive performances, his personal growth, and his unwavering commitment to making a difference, he has become an icon in the world of cinema. His transformative journey not only impacts him but also inspires a new generation of actors and filmmakers to push boundaries and elevate their own artistry. As he continues to evolve, Phoenix's legacy will undoubtedly endure, resonating for years to come and inspiring future generations to embrace their own transformative journeys.

c h a t v a r i e t y . c o m

chatvariety.com

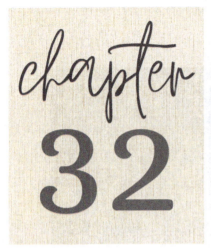
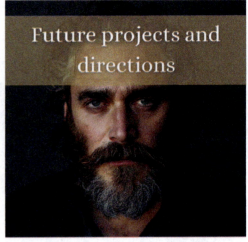

Chapter 32

Future projects and directions

In this chapter, we delve into the exciting realm of Joaquin Phoenix's future projects and explore the directions he may pursue in his career.

As one of the most revered actors of his generation, Joaquin Phoenix has consistently sought out challenging and unconventional roles that push the boundaries of artistic expression. Looking ahead, we find ourselves eagerly anticipating what lies in store for this enigmatic performer.

Phoenix's commitment to his craft and his relentless pursuit of unique and thought-provoking roles make it difficult to predict his future projects with certainty. However, there are a few forthcoming ventures that have already generated considerable buzz within the industry.

c h a t v a r i e t y . c o m

Firstly, there are reports of Phoenix collaborating with visionary director Guillermo del Toro on an eagerly awaited supernatural thriller titled "Shadows of the Soul." With del Toro's mastery of visual storytelling and Phoenix's ability to fully inhabit complex characters, this collaboration promises to be a captivating cinematic experience. The film, set in a hauntingly atmospheric town, explores the thin line between reality and the supernatural. Phoenix's portrayal of a troubled artist plagued by his own creations is poised to be a tour-de-force performance that audiences will eagerly anticipate.

Additionally, rumors have been circulating about Phoenix taking on the challenging role of a historical figure in a biographical drama titled "Unforgotten Legacy." The film delves into the life of an influential figure from the past, shedding light on their struggles, triumphs, and impact on society. Phoenix's ability to fully embody characters and immerse himself in their personas will undoubtedly lend depth and nuance to the portrayal. This project presents an opportunity for Phoenix to explore the complexities of history while bringing forgotten stories to the forefront.

Furthermore, Phoenix has expressed a keen interest in exploring the world of directing. After years of refining his acting skills and collaborating with some of the industry's most notable filmmakers, it comes as no surprise that he wishes to carve out his own path behind the camera. With an astute understanding of storytelling and a meticulous attention to detail, Phoenix's directorial debut holds immense promise. His unique perspective and deeply analytical approach to character development could pave the way for a new era of compelling and visually striking films.

chatvariety.com

In addition to these specific projects, it is essential to highlight Phoenix's dedication to portraying complex, socially relevant characters. Throughout his career, he has been unafraid to tackle narratives that engage with pressing issues such as mental health, social inequality, and personal redemption. This commitment to meaningful storytelling ensures that Phoenix's future projects will likely continue to provoke reflection and spark conversations. He has time and time again used his platform to shed light on important topics and challenge societal norms.

One area where Phoenix's passion for social justice shines through is his activism for environmental and animal rights causes. He has been a vocal advocate for the protection of our planet and the well-being of animals, using his platform to raise awareness and effect change. It wouldn't be surprising if Phoenix makes a foray into producing content that champions his ideals and drives change through media. By aligning his artistic endeavors with his activism, he can create a powerful synergy that amplifies his impact and extends his reach beyond the confines of the screen.

As we eagerly look ahead to the future projects and directions of Joaquin Phoenix, one thing remains certain – he will continue to captivate audiences and push the boundaries of his craft. Whether it's through his intense character portrayals, his passion for social justice, or his venture into directing, Phoenix's artistic journey promises to be a dynamic and transformative one.

chatvariety.com

In conclusion, Chapter 32 delves into the exciting possibilities that await Joaquin Phoenix in his future projects and explores the various directions he may choose to take in his career. With his extraordinary talent, unwavering dedication to his craft, and a commitment to challenging narratives, Joaquin Phoenix's future contributions to the world of cinema are sure to be groundbreaking and awe-inspiring. As audiences, we eagerly await the next chapter in Phoenix's artistic evolution, knowing that whatever he chooses will undoubtedly leave a lasting impact on the world of film and storytelling.

c h a t v a r i e t y . c o m

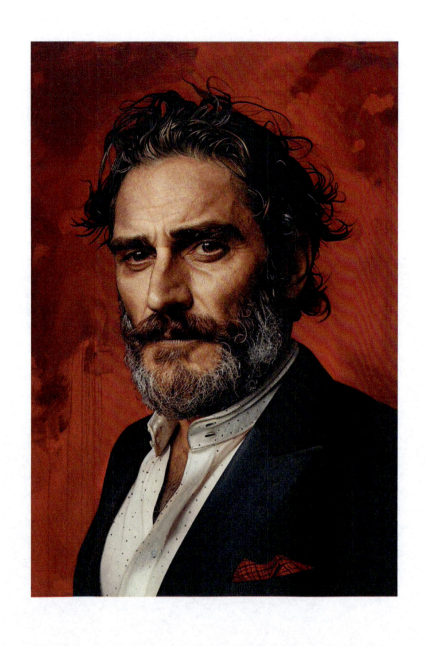

chatvariety.com

CONCLUSION

chatvariety.com

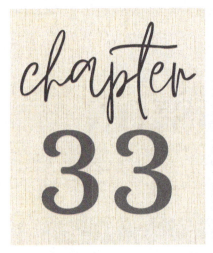
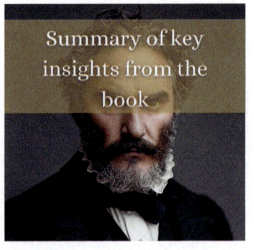

chapter 33

Summary of key insights from the book

Throughout this book, we have delved into the life and career of the remarkable actor, Joaquin Phoenix. From his early years to his rise to fame, his iconic roles, and his off-screen persona, we have explored the multifaceted aspects of his life. Here, in this final chapter, we bring together the key insights garnered from our exploration.

One of the most significant aspects of Joaquin Phoenix's journey is his ability to overcome adversity and reinvent himself. From his early experiences growing up in a family deeply involved in the entertainment industry, Phoenix faced the daunting challenge of carving out his own identity as an actor. While his brother, the late River Phoenix, had already made a name for himself, Joaquin had to navigate his own path and find his unique voice. It was through this struggle that he developed his tenacity, resilience, and unwavering commitment to his craft.

c h a t v a r i e t y . c o m

Phoenix's breakthrough came in the form of his riveting portrayal of Commodus in "Gladiator," which earned him critical acclaim and an Academy Award nomination. This role showcased his ability to embody complex characters with depth and nuance, setting the stage for future transformative performances. Joaquin's commitment to fully immersing himself in a character's psyche was evident in his role as Johnny Cash in "Walk the Line," for which he won an Academy Award. His dedication was unparalleled as he learned to sing and play the guitar like Cash himself, further displaying his ability to masterfully merge his own identity with that of the characters he portrays.

Speaking of roles, our analysis of his landmark films and performances shows that Joaquin Phoenix truly becomes the character he portrays. His deep sense of empathy and emotional intelligence allows him to tap into the essence of each character, bringing them to life on screen. In "The Master," he inhabited the tortured soul of Freddie Quell, capturing the inner turmoil of a troubled war veteran with haunting realism. Similarly, in "Her," his portrayal of Theodore Twombly showcased his ability to portray vulnerability and longing, eliciting profound emotional connections with the audience.

c h a t v a r i e t y . c o m

Beyond his on-screen persona, Joaquin Phoenix's personal life and beliefs hold great significance. He is a man of strong convictions, using his platform to shed light on various societal issues close to his heart. His dedication to animal rights has led him to be a vocal advocate for veganism and an outspoken critic of animal cruelty. In fact, during his Academy Award acceptance speech for "Joker," he used the global platform to highlight important environmental concerns and implore others to embrace compassion and unity. This intersection of art and activism has endeared him to many, as he exemplifies the notion that one's voice and influence can be used to create positive and transformative change.

Collaborations and controversies have also played a role in shaping Phoenix's trajectory. The uniqueness of his working dynamics with directors and fellow actors has led to both fruitful creative endeavors and challenges along the way. His collaborative spirit and willingness to take risks have resulted in successful partnerships with visionary directors like Paul Thomas Anderson and Spike Jonze, resulting in deeply impactful films. However, his uncompromising dedication to his craft has at times caused clashes with filmmakers who may have different visions, highlighting his unwavering commitment to maintaining authenticity and integrity in his work.

c h a t v a r i e t y . c o m

Navigating the complex landscape of Hollywood has required resilience and the ability to find resolutions amidst conflicts, further solidifying his reputation as a dedicated professional. Despite the ever-present trappings of fame, Joaquin Phoenix has remained grounded and focused on his true passion for acting. He continues to pursue roles that challenge the boundaries of storytelling, choosing projects that allow him to inhabit characters from different walks of life and explore the complexities of the human experience. His relentless pursuit of artistic excellence has positioned him as not only one of the most respected actors of his generation but as a trailblazer who has shattered the limitations of what it means to be a modern-day actor.

As we reflect on Joaquin Phoenix's legacy and influence, it becomes evident that his contribution to film and culture is substantial. His ability to transform and evolve as an actor and individual highlights the essence of his career. This transformative journey is symbolized by the phoenix rising from the ashes, representing rebirth and growth. Joaquin's willingness to embrace vulnerability and explore the depths of the human condition through his characters has given audiences a renewed appreciation for the possibilities of cinema as a medium for introspection and empathy.

In the present day, Joaquin Phoenix stands as a revered figure in the film industry. His remarkable journey, filled with personal and professional growth, has captivated audiences and critics alike. Looking ahead, his future projects and directions promise to challenge boundaries, leaving us eagerly awaiting what comes next. It is the combination of his innate talent, unwavering dedication to his craft, and deep understanding of the human experience that positions him as a true artist, capable of leaving a lasting impact on both cinema and society.

c h a t v a r i e t y . c o m

In conclusion, the insights gathered from the exploration of Joaquin Phoenix's life and career showcase the passion, dedication, and resilience that have shaped him into the iconic figure he is today. His impact on cinema and beyond is undeniable, and his story serves as an inspiration for aspiring actors and filmmakers. Joaquin Phoenix's eternal flame will continue to illuminate the world of entertainment, leaving a lasting legacy for generations to come.

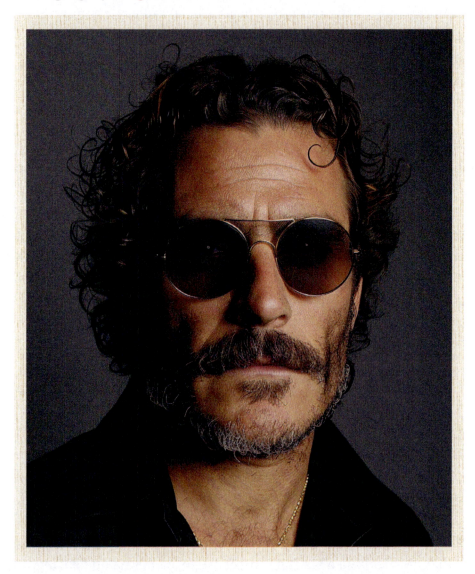

c h a t v a r i e t y . c o m

chatvariety.com

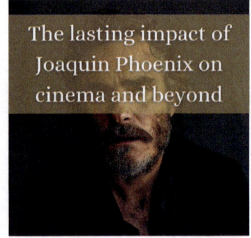

chapter 34

The lasting impact of Joaquin Phoenix on cinema and beyond

Joaquin Phoenix's impact on cinema and the world at large cannot be overstated. Through his unparalleled talent, dedication to his craft, and fearless approach to storytelling, he has left an indelible mark on the industry.

One of the most significant contributions Phoenix has made is his commitment to pushing boundaries and challenging societal norms through his choice of roles. He has consistently sought out characters that test the limits of his acting abilities and explore the complexities of the human experience. From his raw and emotionally charged performance as a troubled teen in "To Die For" to his portrayal of a tormented former soldier in "The Master," Phoenix has fearlessly embraced the darker side of humanity and tackled subjects often shied away from in mainstream cinema.

Phoenix's ability to delve into the depths of a character's psyche and bring their struggles to life is a testament to his extraordinary talent. He immerses himself so fully in each role that it becomes difficult to separate the actor from the character. This dedication to his craft allows him to create authentic and deeply layered performances that resonate with audiences on a profound level.

chatvariety.com

His portrayal of Johnny Cash in "Walk the Line" stands as one of his most transformative performances to date. Phoenix not only mastered Cash's distinctive voice and mannerisms but also tapped into the emotional journey of a music icon battling personal demons. Through his portrayal, he brought a deeper understanding of Cash's turmoil and his eventual redemption, earning Phoenix critical acclaim and an Academy Award nomination for Best Actor.

But it is his portrayal of the Joker in the 2019 film of the same name that truly exemplifies Phoenix's unmatched commitment to his roles. With a physical and emotional transformation so profound it is almost painful to watch, Phoenix delves into the darkest corners of Arthur Fleck's troubled mind. The result is a haunting and harrowing performance that challenges audiences to question the boundaries of empathy and explore the complexities of mental illness.

In addition to his acting prowess, Phoenix's off-screen persona and dedication to social activism have further solidified his impact. Throughout his career, he has used his platform not only to entertain but also to shed light on important social issues. Whether it is advocating for animal rights, speaking out against injustice, or championing environmental sustainability, Phoenix has consistently utilized his influence to make a difference in the world.

His acceptance speech at the 92nd Academy Awards, where he passionately advocated for equality and empathetic understanding, became an iconic moment in the history of the Oscars. Phoenix's authenticity in his beliefs and his earnest commitment to bringing about change resonated with viewers around the world, inspiring them to reevaluate their own actions and beliefs.

chatvariety.com

Furthermore, Phoenix's collaborations with renowned directors and fellow actors have elevated the level of storytelling in the industry. Directors such as Paul Thomas Anderson, Spike Jonze, and Todd Phillips recognize his ability to bring depth and nuance to his characters, resulting in some of the most compelling performances in recent memory.

His collaborations with these talented filmmakers have not only produced remarkable films but have also pushed the boundaries of what cinema can achieve. Phoenix's willingness to take risks and delve into challenging subject matter has opened up new avenues for storytelling, encouraging others in the industry to pursue bold and unconventional narratives.

Beyond the world of cinema, Phoenix's influence extends to the next generation of actors and filmmakers. His dedication and fearlessness serve as an example for aspiring artists, encouraging them to take risks, embrace their uniqueness, and use their craft as a tool for social change. Phoenix's body of work has set a new standard for excellence in acting, inspiring others to push boundaries, challenge societal norms, and tell stories that matter.

c h a t v a r i e t y . c o m

In conclusion, Joaquin Phoenix's impact on cinema and beyond is profound and enduring. His performances have redefined the boundaries of acting, taking audiences on emotional journeys that linger long after the credits roll. His activism has sparked important conversations and inspired individuals to make a difference in the world. Through his talent, dedication, and commitment to using his platform for good, Phoenix continues to leave an indelible mark on both the world of cinema and the hearts of audiences worldwide.

c h a t v a r i e t y . c o m

chatvariety.com

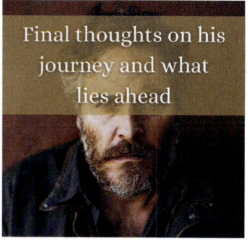

chapter 35

Final thoughts on his journey and what lies ahead

Throughout this book, we have delved deep into the life and career of Joaquin Phoenix, exploring the trials and triumphs that have shaped him into the celebrated actor he is today. As we come to the end of our journey, it is essential to further reflect on the impact he has had on the world of cinema and explore the possibilities that lie ahead for this enigmatic and multifaceted talent.

Joaquin Phoenix's career has been a testament to his unwavering dedication and relentless pursuit of artistic excellence. It is this unwavering commitment to his craft that has propelled him to the forefront of Hollywood's most revered actors. Each role he takes on becomes an opportunity not only to entertain but also to challenge societal norms and ignite conversations about the human condition.

From his early years as a child actor performing alongside his siblings in makeshift street shows, Phoenix displayed an innate talent and an intense desire to make art that resonates with audiences on a profound level. As he grew older, he harnessed this passion, honing his skills in independent films that allowed him to explore the intricacies of complex characters and delve into uncharted emotional territories.

It is Phoenix's exceptional ability to transform himself for each role that sets him apart as one of the most transformative actors of his generation. His physical and emotional metamorphoses are nothing short of astonishing. Whether it is the gaunt figure of Johnny Cash in "Walk the Line" or the emaciated, unhinged Arthur Fleck in "Joker," Phoenix commits himself entirely to the characters he portrays, leaving audiences utterly captivated and immersed in the worlds he creates.

But beyond his transformative abilities lies a deep well of empathy and understanding. Phoenix possesses a remarkable gift for exploring the depths of human emotions, uncovering the rawest vulnerabilities, and showcasing the humanity that resides within even the most troubled souls. He is a master at exposing the nuances of pain, joy, love, and despair, allowing audiences to connect with his characters on a visceral level and walk away from each performance with a greater understanding of the human experience.

Moreover, Joaquin Phoenix's career has been intertwined with a passionate commitment to making a difference in the world. His advocacy for animal rights and environmental conservation has become an integral part of his public persona. Through his documentary "Earthlings" and his involvement with organizations like PETA, Phoenix has become a prominent voice in raising awareness about the cruelty inflicted upon animals and the urgent need for sustainable living. His dedication to these causes extends beyond the screen, as evidenced by his passionate speeches and activism surrounding climate change.

Looking to the future, the trajectory of Joaquin Phoenix's career promises continued exhilaration and artistic exploration. His affinity for selecting challenging and thought-provoking roles suggests that he will seek out projects that push boundaries, challenge societal conventions, and shed light on aspects of the human experience that often go unnoticed. With his immense talent and unwavering dedication, there is no doubt that his performances will continue to captivate, inspire, and incite conversations for generations to come.

Additionally, the collaborative possibilities for Joaquin Phoenix are limitless. His magnetic presence and reputation for delivering transformative performances have attracted acclaimed directors and fellow actors eager to work with him. The prospect of witnessing his creative energy merge with that of other industry powerhouses is nothing short of awe-inspiring. Each collaboration has the potential to push the boundaries of storytelling, providing audiences with unforgettable cinematic experiences that blur the lines between reality and fiction.

As Joaquin Phoenix steps into the next phase of his career, it is certain that he will continue to captivate and inspire audiences. His relentless pursuit of truth, his ability to fully inhabit and understand his characters, and his unwavering commitment to making a difference make him a force to be reckoned with. The impact of his performances will undoubtedly leave an indelible mark on the art of storytelling, shaping the future of cinema and serving as a reminder of the transformative power of the human spirit.

chatvariety.com

In conclusion, Joaquin Phoenix's journey has been one of resilience, reinvention, and artistic brilliance. From his early struggles to his rise to fame, he has shown us the power of perseverance, passion, and compassion. His unwavering commitment to his craft, combined with his desire to make a positive impact on the world, sets him apart as not just an actor but as a true artist and humanitarian. Let us eagerly await the projects he will choose, the collaborations he will embark upon, and the emotions he will continue to provoke in audiences worldwide. Joaquin Phoenix's legacy is one that will endure, inspiring future generations of actors to explore the depths of their artistry and use their platform for social change.

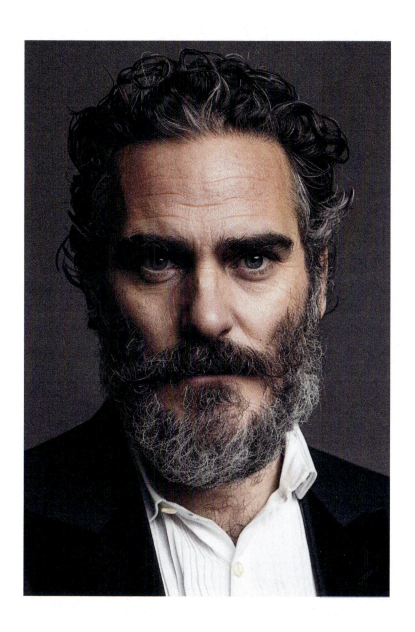

chatvariety.com

Printed in Great Britain
by Amazon